ACUPRESSURE
FOR
WOMEN
CATHRYN BAUER

ACUPRESSURE
F O R
W O M E N
CATHRYN BAUER

Illustrated by Ann Weston

Well-Woman Series
Edited by Margot Edwards

The Crossing Press, Freedom, CA 95019

The information in this book does not constitute medical advice. Not every suggestion applies to your particular case. Consult a trusted health professional if questions arise.

Printed in the U.S.A. by McNaughton and Gunn of Ann Arbor, Michigan

Cover illustration by Rowan Silverberg
Cover design by Betsy Bayley and Elizabeth Palmer

Library of Congress Cataloging-in-Publication Data

Bauer, Cathryn.
    Acupressure for women.

    (Well-woman series)
    Bibliography: p.
    Includes index.
    1. Acupressure. 2. Women–Diseases–Treatment.
3. Women–Health and hygiene.   I. Title.   II. Series.
RM723.A27B38   1987   618   87-5440
ISBN 0-89594-233-X
ISBN 0-89594-232-1 (pbk.)

This book is dedicated to the memory of two women:
Susan Shackman Levine whose enthusiasm did so much to carry it
through to completion;
and my grandmother, Elsie. "The lines have fallen for me in pleasant
places; I have a goodly heritage." (Ps. 16)

ACKNOWLEDGEMENTS

I have received a great deal of valuable assistance in the preparation of *Acupressure for Women.*

I am very grateful to Elaine Goldman Gill of Crossing Press for the attention and interest which she has given my work. Margot Edwards, Editor of the Well Woman series, went far beyond the call of duty in helping me to put my ideas into print. Her enthusiasm and skill continually inspire me. Thanks to Ann Weston for the charts and drawings which enrich and clarify the text. It was a privilege — and a fine education — to work with each of these women.

I would like to express my appreciation to my first Acupressure teacher, Michael Gach, whose patience and support helped me to persevere. Gratitude is also due to Dianne Connelly, Ph.D., M.Ac., and David Ford, C.A., who introduced me to the Five Elements Theory. I am deeply grateful to each of the anonymous "nurses, witches, and midwives" who kept natural healing methods alive through the centuries, often at grave personal cost.

Throughout the writing of this book, I was enriched by the friendship and support of Robin Cowan, Hedy Babka, Edward Spencer, Mary Nett, Robert Price, Brother Isaiah Teichert and Lindsay Roberts. I would also like to thank the community of St. Albert's Priory in Oakland, California for their Gregorian chant, hospitality and prayers; Marge and Dana Hagerty, who have inspired and encouraged me for many years and my friends at the College of Chemistry, University of California at Berkeley.

I am most grateful to my husband, Theodore Kahn, for our life together.

CONTENTS

Preface 1

Introduction—What Acupressure Can Do For You 3

Chapter 1—The Western View 11

Chapter 2—The Asian View 15

Chapter 3—Premenstrual Syndrome 37

Chapter 4—Pregnancy, Birth and Nursing 71

Chapter 5—Menopause and Aging 109

Appendix I—Glossary 138

Appendix II—Index of Pressure Points 142

Appendix III—Recommended Reading 144

PREFACE

This book developed out of my work as an Acupressure practitioner. I noticed that women clients had better results when they followed up my work with Acupressure self-care. To teach them their homework, I sought out instructional materials, without success. As my practice grew and I began to give classes, my collection of charts and instructions expanded, developing into this book.

Earlier, a personal experience taught me the benefits of Acupressure self-treatment. After an auto accident, I was left with a blood clot and serious neuromuscular damage to one leg. An orthopedist pronounced my limp and chronic pain to be incurable. Unwilling to accept this, I promptly initiated a program of self-treatment which included Acupressure, visualization, prayer and Tai Chi Chu'an. Acupressure relieved my pain and stimulated the healing process to the extent that I eventually regained complete use of my leg.

My own case demonstrates that our bodies and minds contain potential for regeneration. This potential extends far beyond the "logical" perceptions of Western medical practitioners, although it can work hand in hand with medical treatment. If you're willing to learn the rudiments of an ancient skill and use it in your best interests, you'll discover that Acupressure will prove its value as a stimulant to your body's vast resources.

INTRODUCTION

What Acupressure Can Do For You

Acupressure is an age-old therapy which is easy to learn and even easier to use. You can give yourself a treatment almost anywhere. Your only tools are your fingers, your knowledge and concentration. You can use Acupressure self-treatment for relief of symptoms such as menstrual cramps or water retention. You can also use Acupressure as a means of strengthening and balancing your body's deep energies for optimal well-being of your body, mind and spirit.

Acupressure had its origins in ancient China. It began with the observation that when you are hurt, your hand instinctively moves to cover the injury. This generally provides a slight degree of pain relief. The Chinese sages and physicians carried this awareness further. They found that applying fingertip pressure at specific points on the body consistently helped to calm anxiety and fright, ease the pains of childbirth, and provide relief for many other symptoms of dis-ease.

Conventional treatment does not always provide workable answers for problems such as: "Why do I get colds every winter?" "How can I keep this yeast infection from coming back?" "I can't get any sleep because of these hot flashes." "I wish that I had more energy."

There are no simple answers to these broad health questions, but you'll understand more about the way your body works if you study Acupressure self-help. Healthcare today is in the midst of a transformation. Women themselves are entering the health professions in increasing numbers, and, as practitioners, are paying attention of our special needs. Women as consumers of healthcare are making informed decisions about medical treatment.

As the philosophy of health changes, there is a growing respect for previously unacknowledged healing methods like herbology (plants were the first medicines), biofeedback (taken from Eastern meditation techniques) and the touch therapies—massage, Acupuncture, Acupressure and Shiatsu. With massage, muscles are stroked or kneaded with oil or soothing lotion. In Acupuncture, fine gold or silver needles are inserted into the skin at specific points. With Acupressure, fingertip pressure is applied to Acupuncture points. Shiatsu is the Japanese counterpoint of Acupressure.

If you decide to begin an Aucpressure self-help program, you must be careful to select healthcare professionals who encourage your interest. Progressive professionals now recognize the balancing effect of the touch therapies. They know that Acupressure is a legitimate alternative to the use of prescribed drugs. While a course of medication may be indicated, there are sometimes distressing side effects. Symptoms can reappear when the drug is discontinued. Sedatives and narcotics are potentially addictive. Drugs of almost any kind are considered a threat to the unborn child.

There are differing perspectives on the reasons why the touch therapies are effective. The Asian view suggests that you are healthy when your life-energy is strong and balanced. The Western viewpoint changed in the last half of the twentieth century, and we are finally acknowledging that relaxation is the cornerstone of healthy living. Stress has been identified as the culprit in a wide variety of symptoms. This recognition has led to a new interest in Acupressure as an adjunct—not a replacement—for medical science.

Health is. . .

- Recognizing that you too are an expert with regard to your well being
- Developing awareness of your physical and emotional patterns so that you can respond appropriately
- Allowing dis-ease to be a learning experience
- Taking charge of your life experience, rather than just following along with what happens
- Feeling confident that you can take care of yourself
- Maintaining close and satisfying human relationships
- Having a livelihood which you perceive as meaningful service.
- Regarding your problems as opportunities for personal growth.

How To Work With Acupressure Points

Wash your hands before you apply Acupressure. Make sure they are dry and warm before you apply pressure to a point. It is important to remember that you are doing more than pressing a button. You are relieving pain and tension. You are also balancing energy. Work with a slow and careful touch, particularly if you are not feeling well.

A good beginning is simply to hold your hand over the general area of the point. Let it rest there while you take a deep, relaxed breath. Using the tip of your index finger, approach the specific point location slowly. Move your finger around the area, probing gently until you feel a slight dip that identifies the Acupressure point. Press in lightly, holding a point until you feel the tissues underneath your fingertip soften and relax. Then, press into the point very slowly, until you sense further pressure would require force.

Pay careful attention to what is happening beneath your fingertip. Acupressure points often become warm to your touch, a sign of releasing tension. As you press into the point, note any changes in your breathing. Slower breathing is a sign that you're beginning to relax.

The point is completely released when it's neither warm or cool in temperature and pulsing steadily. The pulsation is similar to the pulse in your wrists and neck, but not as strong. When the point has released, ease your fingertip off slowly. An abrupt release of pressure feels uncomfortable.

Avoid two common mistakes, inaccurate point location and applying pressure for too brief a period of time. Study the charts in each chapter. Accurate point location is a learned skill. Give yourself permission to be a beginner! If you feel relaxed or experience symptomatic relief after a self-treatment session, you are successfully applying the art. Keep practicing to develop sensitivity to the process. Don't be concerned if you take a while to find points. Acupressure self-care is a skill which will serve you well—for the rest of your life.

Precautions

If you are sick, tired or weak, be sure to use a very gentle and gradual touch. Acupressure should never be applied directly to wounds, bruises or sprains. However, you can use Acupressure points near the affected part to increase circulation and relieve muscular stiffness.

There are points which you should not press if you are pregnant, noted throughout the text. Their use can result in prenatal problems.

Acupressure is not a substitute for medical care. If you are ill or injured, consult a licensed M.D. whom you trust. You must also receive regular pelvic exams and pap smears from a doctor or nurse practitioner. In addition, check your breasts for lumps the day after your menstrual period. Your doctor or nurse practitioner will show you how.

If you ever press Acupressure points on someone else, ask their permission first and use a gentle touch.

Acupressure Self-Treatment

You have a lot to gain from taking time to care for yourself. You live in a noisy, rapidly-paced society which demands a great deal from you. You are constantly being asked to produce and give of yourself, which drains energy. Make a conscious effort to replenish this energy daily. There are times when it's best to receive Acupressure from someone else. If you're feeling tired and overextended, have a professional or a friend take care of you with Acupressure. If you know someone who shares your interest in Acupressure, take turns working with each other. Also check the classified section of your neighborhood newspaper for professional Acupressure practitioners. Contact bodywork schools advertised in health-oriented magazines. Their staff will refer you to graduates who practice in your area.

Acupressure self-treatment includes other holistic modalities. Throughout this book, there are references to nutrition, exercise and the use of herbs and other traditional remedies that make Acupressure treatment more effective. If you use herbal remedies, be certain that you read and understand the directions. These are different for each herb. You may also be interested in exploring mental techniques for healing, such as affirmation and visualization.

Yeshi Donden, holistic physician to the Dalai Lama of Tibet, encourages his students to develop a perception of the universe as a place where healing is possible. This outlook is your best possible supplement to Acupressure self-care or any other form of health treatment.

Visualization

Visualization is a helpful tool for "programming" yourself for happiness and health. It involves using your imagination to create pictures of yourself exactly as you would like to be, free of dis-ease and feeling better about yourself. Visualization, like affirmation, creates a different frame of mind which makes desired change possible. You will have the best results if you practice daily.

Below is an example of visualization practice. You can try it (or any part of it) to see how to originate your own visualizations. You may find it helpful to read the following instructions into a tape recorder, using a calm and relaxed voice. Play back when you are ready to practice the techniques.

Begin by establishing a relaxed state. Take three long, deep breaths. Allow yourself to be aware of what you are feeling as you inhale and exhale. How do you feel as you breathe? What is the temperature of the air that you draw into your nostrils? Feel your chest rising and falling. Feel the little pause between your inhalation and exhalation. Continuing to relax and breathe deeply, count backward from ten to one.

Now that you are relaxed and centered, allow yourself to form a mental picture. See yourself looking and feeling exactly as you'd like be. Let the picture of a healthy, confident, successful self be as complete as you can make it. (This will become progressively easier with practice.) Hold onto this image as long as you wish.

When you feel finished, open your eyes slowly. Again, concentrate on taking deep, relaxed breaths. Be aware of the way you feel and how this has changed since the beginning of your visualization.

©'87 A.Weston

Affirmations

Affirmations are short statements which help you to create a positive mental attitude. You can use affirmations to build a frame of mind which makes it possible to have, do or be what you want. Affirmations should be spoken, sung or written every day. The key to using affirmations successfully is patient repetition.

Some examples:

- My body is strong and relaxed.
- I know that the world is a safe and happy place for me.
- I now forgive myself (or someone else) for_____
- My skin is perfect, healthy and clear.
- I now allow a deep, regular sleep.
- I process dis-ease effectively.
- I am alive with interest in life.
- I constantly experience the love of God (a higher powerthe universe.)
- I now allow a close and loving relationship with _____

Affirmations may be repeated when you are applying Acupressure self-treatment.

CHAPTER ONE

The Western Viewpoint

The Western viewpoint suggests that Acupressure techniques stimulate the body's own resources for healing by influencing the nervous system. The Acupressure process somehow modifies the action of stress-related hormones and interferes with the transmission of pain. Although research reports are scattered, they all support the use of non-pharmaceutical therapies that enhance relaxation. For example, researchers at the Harvard Medical School discovered that regular relaxation practice decreased the body's response to norepinephrine, one of the "fight or flight" hormones which elevates the blood pressure and contributes to hypertension.[1] Hypertension was one of the first "dis-eases of civilization" identified by pioneers like Hans Selye, M.D. who defined stress as "wear and tear" upon the body and mind. Selye put forth a "fight-flight" theory in the fifties that became the baseline of today's wider understanding of stress related illness.[2]

When you're angry and afraid, your "fight or flight" reflex stimulates a variety of physical responses, most of them unpleasant. Your heart pounds. Your blood pressure rises. Your mouth gets dry and your muscles tighten, enabling you to run away. While these responses were essential to human survival in the past, they are inappropriate for life today. You can seldom solve job or domestic problems by fighting or running away. Yet, as long as you feel threatened, your body remains in "fight or flight mode" until the situation is resolved. You can remain in this mode for a period of less than a minute or it can continue for many years. Chronic, unmitigated stress is strongly associated with illnesses like gastric ulcer and hypertension.[3]

A psychologist at Duke University Medical Center, Dr. Richard Surwit, used relaxation techniques with diabetic patients. He found that relaxation heightened his subjects' ability to regulate blood sugar levels. This is a significant finding, as the body's inability to control the blood sugar ultimately causes damage.[4] Researchers at the Preventive Medicine Research Institute in San Francisco found that relaxation lowered bloodstream cholesterol levels and lessened the severity of angina attacks.[5, 6]

Stress reduction research suggests that Acupressure is a valuable tool in a stress management program. Stress reduction techniques emphasize slow, deep breathing to induce relaxation. There are Acupressure points in the chest and upper back to reduce chest constriction and shallow breathing. You can also press points to relieve joint stiffness and other discomforts. Indirectly, Acupressure can reduce insomnia, depression and pain.[7]

Health professionals are reaching a better understanding of the way that touch therapies help you withstand the pressures of daily life. They also observe many situations where touch therapies ease the shock of illness or injury. Hans Selye suggests that your experience of pain is strongly affected by your feelings that accompany discomfort. Panic and uncertainty increase tension. Tension, in turn, heightens pain perception. Tension also raises your blood pressure which can aggravate the uncomfortable fight/flight symptoms. If you can remain calm and relaxed with Acupressure, your pain symptoms do not have to disrupt your life totally. Touch therapies do interfere with pain transmission. Dr. David Bresler, Director of the Pain Control Unit at the University of California, Los Angeles Medical Center, quotes studies which indicate that Acupressure points are really "neural receptors." These receptors, located on the surface of the skin, are highly sensitive to stimulation, be it the touch of a finger or an acupuncturist's needle. Both stimulate changes in heart rate, blood flow, endocrine function and the immune system. Dr. Bresler found stimulation of Acupressure points to be particularly effective with musculoskeletal pain, migraines and nerve damage. Bresler successfully used Acupuncture treatment for chronic depression and anxiety.[8]

Dr. Bruce Pomeranz, a zoologist at the University of Toronto, suggests that stimulation of the "neural receptors" reduces pain by causing your brain to release endorphins, the body's natural painkillers (structurally related to morphine). Although researchers still have not established the exact mechanisms which make pain medication effective, it is widely theorized that endorphins, morphine and related substances do not provide direct pain relief. Instead, they stimulate your body's mechanism for "switching off" pain — the inhibitory and excitatory pleasure centers located in the brain.[9]

Your inhibitory pleasure system gives you the ability to feel relaxed, secure and positive about yourself. When it is inactivated, you are prone to emotional upset and the appearance of stress symptoms. You have a stronger-than-usual response to physical and emotional stimuli. You are "thin-skinned" and easily affected by annoying input. If you have uncomfortable symptoms, they tend to be aggravated by the resulting tension. Many women experience this as a part of Premenstrual Syndrome (see Chapter Three).

Bresler observed that when your inhibitory pleasure system is activated, you are less likely to suffer emotional discomfort and pain. Pressing Acupressure points may stimulate action of your inhibitory pleasure system. Acupressure might also stimulate your excitatory pleasure system, increasing feelings of confidence and mastery. If you have suffered an injury, like a fracture and your excitatory pleasure system is activated, the accident is less traumatic. You can cope with pain better and trust those assisting you to do what is necessary for your well-being.

In 1986, a ski instructor told me that ski rescue teams in the Colorado Rockies are taught "hands-on" techniques for lessening trauma at the scene of an accident. As the team reaches an injured skier, one member removes her gloves and warms her hands by rubbing them together. She makes direct skin contact with the injured skier, placing one hand on the back of the neck and gently stroking the face with her other hand. It is possible that the rescuer's touch stimulates the neural receptors (Acupressure points), activating both the inhibitory and excitatory pleasure systems that release endorphins.[10]

The avalanche of stress research influences the way that people take care of themselves. Now that "stress" is an everyday word, you hear warnings on every side to reduce stress in your life or suffer the results. Yet, a life without stress is a life without challenge or personal growth. If you live a productive yet stressful lifestyle, you need a consciously planned program of stress reduction. The Western view now includes the use of Acupressure.

Reference Notes

1. Goleman, Daniel, "Relaxation Training Helps the Body Heal," *San Francisco Chronicle*, August 6, 1986.
2. Selye, Hans, M.D., *THE PHYSIOLOGY AND PATHOLOGY OF EXPOSURE TO STRESS*, Acta, 1950.
3. Pelletier, Kenneth R., M.D., *MIND AS HEALER, MIND AS SLAYER*, Delta, 1977.
4. Surwit, Richard, M.D. and Feinglos, Michael, M.D., "Relaxation-Induced Improvement in Glucose Tolerance is Associated with Decreased Plasma Cortisol," *Diabetes Care*, March-April 1984.
5. Jacob, Robert G. "Modifying Neurogenic Components of Hypertension: Relaxation and Biofeedback Therapy," *Maryland State Medical Journal*, March 1984.
6. Ornish, Dean, M.D. *STRESS, DIET AND YOUR HEART*, Holt, Rinehart and Winston, 1982.
7. Namikoshi, Tokujiro. *SHIATSU: JAPANESE FINGER-PRESSURE THERAPY*, Japan Publications, 1969.
8. Bresler, David E., M.D., et al., *FREE YOURSELF FROM PAIN*, Simon and Schuster, Inc., 1979.
9. Pomeranz, Bruce, M.D., "Do Endorphins Mediate Acupuncture Analgesia?" *Advances in Biochemical Psychopharmacology*, August 1978.
10. Personal Interview, January 1986.

CHAPTER TWO
The Eastern View

Acupressure originated from the Taoist philosophy that began centuries ago in China. Having seen how touch could relieve the pain from an injury, the Chinese physicians and philosophers discovered that life-energy flows through the body in twelve defined paths or meridians. When you are healthy, the flow proceeds unblocked, and energy is well distributed throughout the meridian pathways.

The theory was reinforced in modern times by Dr. Kim Bong-han, a professor of medicine at Korea's Pyongyang University. He found that variations in the skin's electrical resistance could be traced along the meridians as they were illustrated in ancient texts. Further research showed that skin cells along the meridians were structurally different from other skin cells. Furthermore, at certain points, there were clusters of these "meridian cells." Classic Chinese medical texts show that the clusters were located at Acupressure points.[1]

Each point has a name and number to identify its effect or location (see Appendix II, Index of Pressure Points). When you apply fingertip pressure to the point, you influence the energy in its meridian in addition to relieving symptoms. You also facilitate a balance of energy among the twelve meridians which manifests itself as whole-person wellness. Dis-ease is a sign that the energy within the meridians is out of balance.

Physicians who developed Acupressure believed that human beings are an integral part of the universe. This concept is the heart of Taoist thinking. Human beings, trees, clouds, land forms, and animals are all part of one substance, one fabric. As such, humans are subject to the laws of nature. Like the physical universe, they continually move through a yearly cycle. When they adapt to the changing cycle, living according to each season, they are healthy and productive. (An example of adaptation is wearing warm clothing during the wintertime.) When they fail to adapt, they are more susceptible to illness.

Chinese philosophers believed in a five-season year. They associated each season with one of five elements which compose the universe. Since you are a part of the natural universe, you are also composed of the elements. Each element is a part of your being, just as it is a part of the world in which you live. When your Five Elements are in harmony, you are balanced and healthy.

Each element has a character of its own. It is connected with an emotion, a taste and a sound, in addition to certain meridians. When an element is out of balance, you are likely to experience one or more specific dis-eases related to that particular element. For example, you might have menstrual cramps. First-aid Acupressure can give you temporary relief from the muscular tension and pain. However, it is likely that your cramps will continue to be a monthly problem until you treat the underlying imbalance in that particular element.

THE FIVE ELEMENTS THEORY

Your Water Element

The Water element is your storehouse of reserve energy to be used when you're under prolonged stress or in crisis. The Water meridians are the Bladder and Kidney. The Kidney meridian stores energy reserves for emergency use, and the Bladder meridian regulates fluid distribution. Your body is as much as eighty percent fluid, an amazing collection of tides and flows that must be balanced by Water. Water is also associated with your sense of hearing (taking in and remembering information), bone health and your sexuality.

The Water emotion, fear, enables you to withdraw for self protection. The ability to pull back in your own interest promotes your survival. However, you can go too far and be "frozen with fear," unable to move on to realize your ambitions. In this case, your voice is fear-full, sounding like a groan or a whine. Since Water governs bone health, you may refer to a frightening experience as "bone-chilling."

The colors of Water are blue and black, the "cool" colors. The Water taste is salty. Salt in excess causes fluid retention. The Water season is Winter when the earth is at rest. Some animals hibernate for a long winter sleep and most people need more sleep during the Winter months.

Symptoms and illnesses associated with Water imbalance include: cold hands and feet, PMS, brittle hair, fractures which are slow to heal, salt cravings, urinary and bladder infections, phobias, earache, low back pain, infertility, and pain and tension along the Water meridians.

See pages 22 and 23 for Kidney and Bladder Meridians.

Your Wood Element

Wood governs the health of the muscles, tendons and ligaments. When wood is in balance, joints move easily and effortlessly. The Wood meridians are the Gall Bladder and Liver. The Liver assimilates food and purifies your blood. The Gall Bladder secretes bile to aid digestion and distributes energy (from foods you eat) throughout your meridians. Wood is related to strong, adaptable eyes and the sense of inner vision, the ability to see different sides of a situation.

Anger is the Wood emotion, an energizer that propels you into constructive action. If Wood is out of balance, you may frequently overreact with any angry response. The sound of Wood is shouting, and its taste is sour. If you frequently crave dill pickles or green olives, you may have a Wood imbalance. Wood colors are purple and green, the traditional colors of healing and transformation.

The season of Wood is Spring, a time of life renewal when you grow as a person and let go of habits and ideas that no longers work for you. Wood gives you energy to reach out to get what you want from life. If Wood is healthy, you can celebrate the aging process without regret.

Symptoms and illnesses associated with Wood imbalance include: headaches, spinal problems, bursitis, muscular spasms, indecision, allergies, tendonitis, eye problems, migraine, chronic rage, and tension and pain along the Wood meridians.

See pages 24 and 25 for Gall Bladder and Liver Meridians.

Your Fire Element

Fire is related to creativity and spark and governs the well-being of your heart. The Fire element has four meridians: Heart, Pericardium, Small Intestine and Triple Warmer. The Heart meridian (Supreme Controller) regulates blood circulation and oversees the meridian system. The Pericardium meridian (Heart Protector) absorbs blows that could damage your heart. The Small Intestine processes food, attracting nutrients and discarding wastes. The Triple Warmer protects and regulates your "Three Burning Spaces," chest, solar plexus and abdomen. An energy presence without physical form, the Triple Warmer is the only meridian without a corresponding organ.

The emotion associated with Fire is joy. When Fire is in balance, you have a greater capacity to feel pleasure and excitement ("on fire with enthusiasm"). Laughter is the sound of Fire, and your ability to enjoy a good laugh is an indicator of health. Humor which mocks or degrades others, however, shows an imbalance.

The taste associated with Fire is bitter. Frequent cravings for unsweetened chocolate and strong, black coffee or tea indicates imbalance. Fire colors are red and pink. They can "cheer you up" or make you feel "like a neon sign." If your wardrobe contains only drab shades, or is composed entirely of red and pink, there may be a Fire imbalance. The Fire season is Summer, the traditional vacation time. Like many people, you may find relief from chronic physical or emotional problems when you travel to a summery climate. However, being happy and well only in the warm months — or not being able to handle warm wearther — are signs of imbalance.

Symptoms and dis-eases associated with Fire imbalance include: heart trouble, poor circulation, lack of sexual desire, depression, body temperature changes, skin changes, insensitivity to others, apathy ("losing heart"), and tension or pain along Fire meridians.

See pages 26, 27, 28, and 29 for Heart,Pericardium, Small Intestine and Triple Warmer Meridians.

Your Earth Element

The Earth element is your base. It gives you physical and emotional balance and, with the Water element, creates your sexuality and fertility. Spleen and Stomach are the Earth's meridians. The Spleen builds blood, and the Stomach digests food. Together, they regulate the menstrual cycle, the digestive process and emotional reaction patterns.

Sympathy is the emotion associated with Earth. With imbalance, you can be stuck in giving too much sympathy at your own expense and excusing inappropriate behavior in yourself and others. You may also ignore your own or others' needs. A balanced Earth gives you the sense of stability, belonging wherever you are. Earth regulates your physical and emotional cycles, helping you adapt to your natural rhythms. When Earth is in balance, you understand that some days are more productive than others.

Singing is the sound of Earth. An Earth-imbalanced voice sounds like a song without a tune. Singing helps to balance your Earth meridians. The taste of Earth is sweet. With imbalance, you crave sweets, even after you've conquered a white sugar habit. The season of Earth is Late Summer, a period marked by weather changes. When Earth is in balance, you can enjoy any day, whatever the weather. Yellow, orange and brown are Earth colors.

Symptoms and illnesses associated with Earth imbalance include: canker sores, stomach/abdominal pain, ulcers, nausea and vomiting, eating disorders, diabetes, yeast infections, PMS infertility, irregular ovulation, hypoglycemia, self-pity, mood swings, and tension and pain along the Earth meridians.

See pages 30 and 31 for Spleen and Stomach Meridians.

The Metal Element

The Metal meridians are the Large Intestine and the Lung, and together they determine the health of your bowels, skin and respiration. The Large Intestine which refines and filters food products is a great mover, enabling you to get rid of physical and emotional waste. When Metal is out of balance, foods may affect you badly, and you develop acne, hives or eczema. The Lung meridian controls your breathing. When your breath is slow and regular, you're relaxed.

Grief is the emotion of Metal. If your energy is stuck in Metal, you are continually mourning the past, unable to move ahead and resolve old experiences. Your voice has a weeping sound. Metal is also related to your ability to acquire money and the material goods necessary for survival. Metal colors are white, silver and gray, mourning colors of several Asian societies. The taste of Metal is spicy. With imbalance, you may overuse or avoid pepper, salsa and other spicy condiments.

The Metal season is Autumn, a time of completion and transformation. The Metal element helps you release painful experiences and replace them with hope. Metal is associated with spiritual life, inspiring you to develop a sense of justice and honor. Symptoms and dis-ease associated with Metal imbalance include: acne, eczema, frontal headache, sinus problems, colds and bronchitis, dry or chapped skin, constipation or diarrhea, delayed menstruation, asthma, pain and tension along the Metal meridians.

See pages 32 and 33 for the Large Intestine and Lung Meridians.

The Governing Vessel and the Conception Vessel

The Governing Vessel and the Conception Vessel are extra meridians which serve as reservoirs for excess energy. They comprise a binding network which draws energy from the Kidney meridian for distribution throughout the body. Pressing points on the extra meridians calms and strengthens you, increasing the benefits derived from pressing points on the organ meridians.

See pages 34 and 35 for the Governing Vessel and Conception Vessel.

The Kidney Meridian

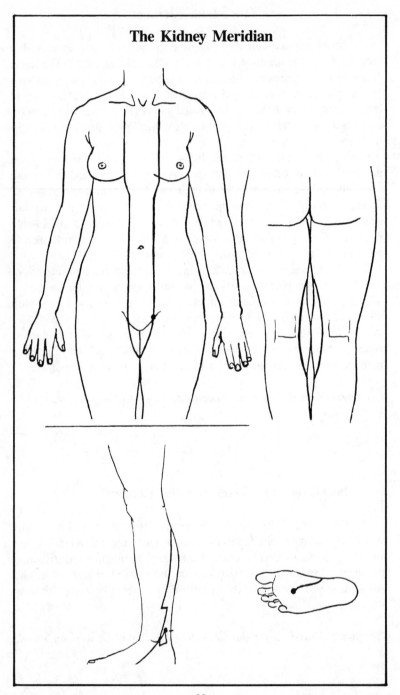

The Bladder Meridian

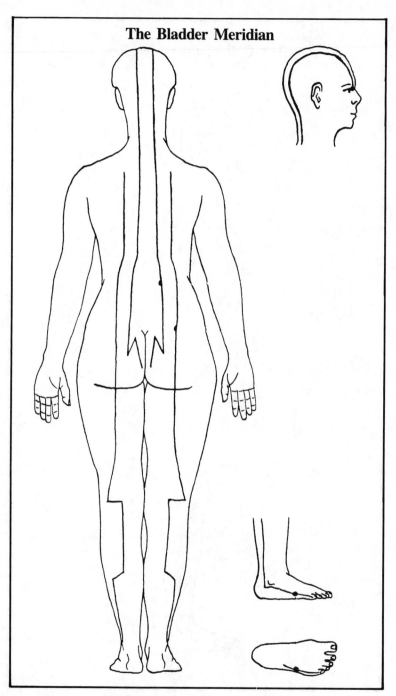

The Gall Bladder Meridian

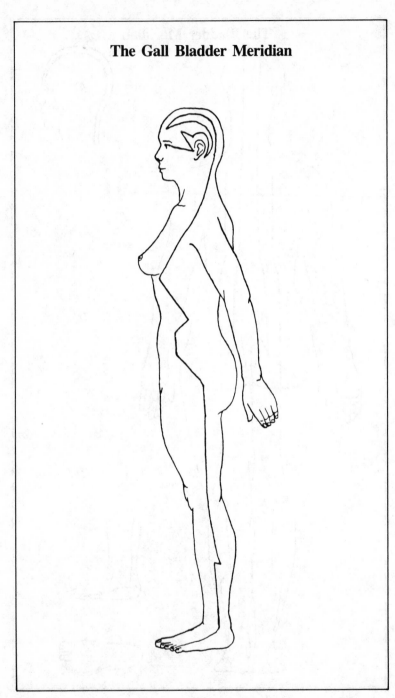

The Liver Meridian

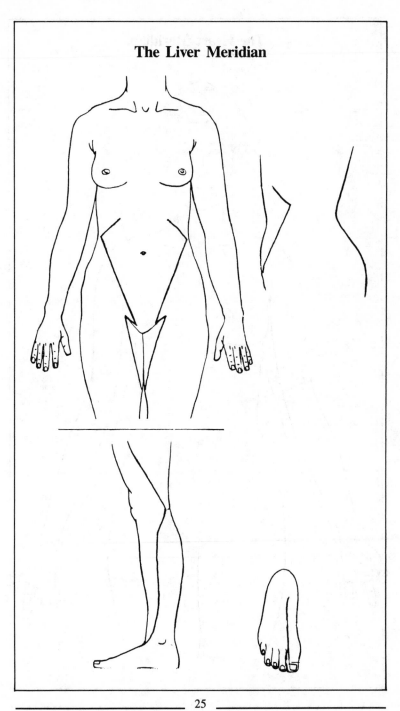

The Heart Meridian.

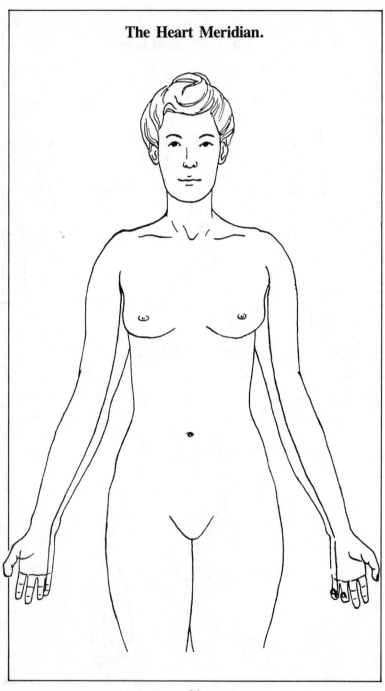

The Pericardium Meridian.

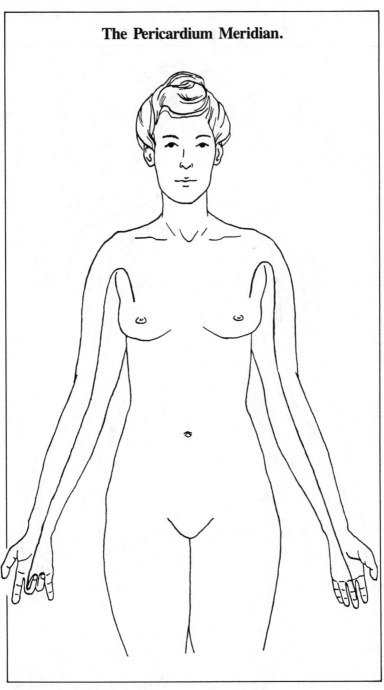

The Small Intestine Meridian.

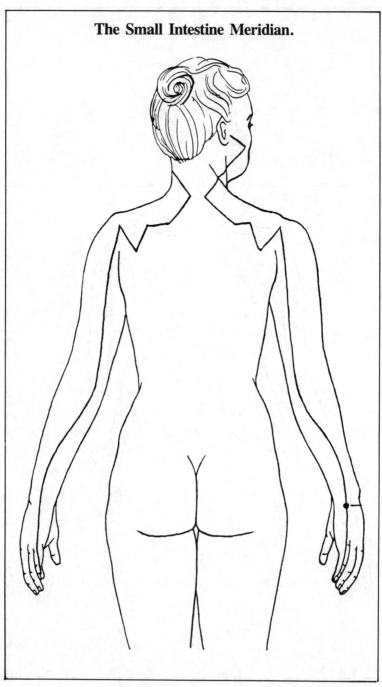

The Triple Warmer Meridian.

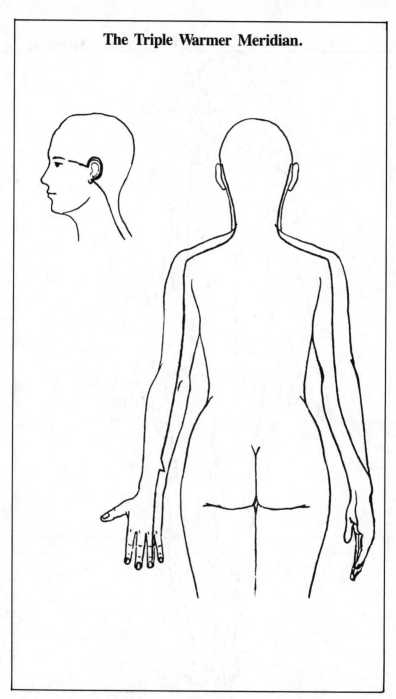

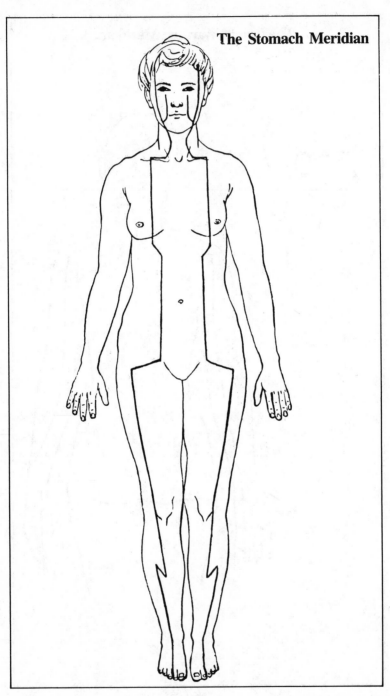

The Stomach Meridian

The Spleen Meridian

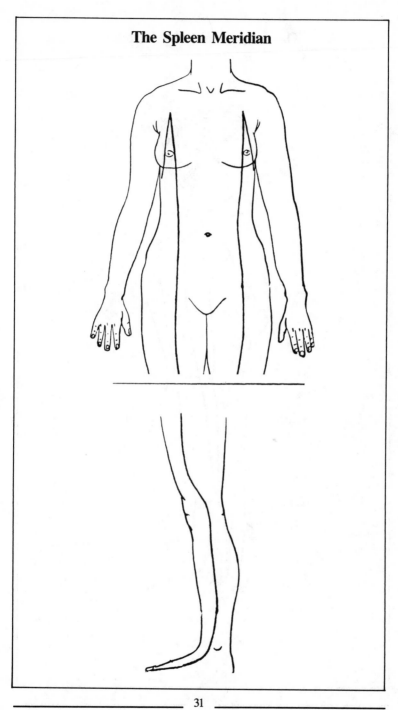

The Large Intestine Meridian

The Lung Meridian

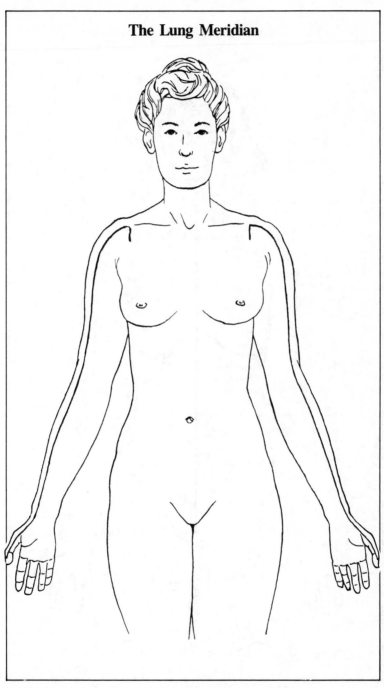

Conception Vessel

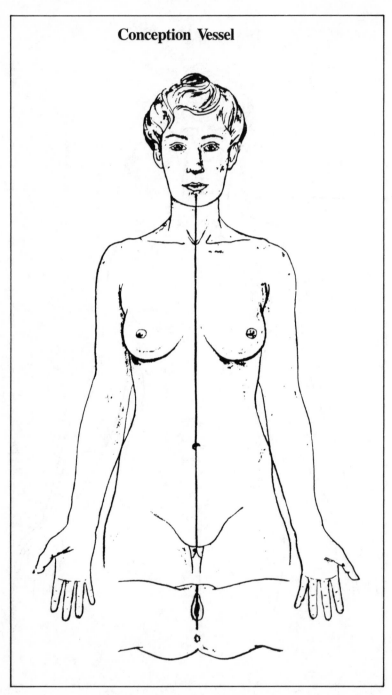

Governing Vessel

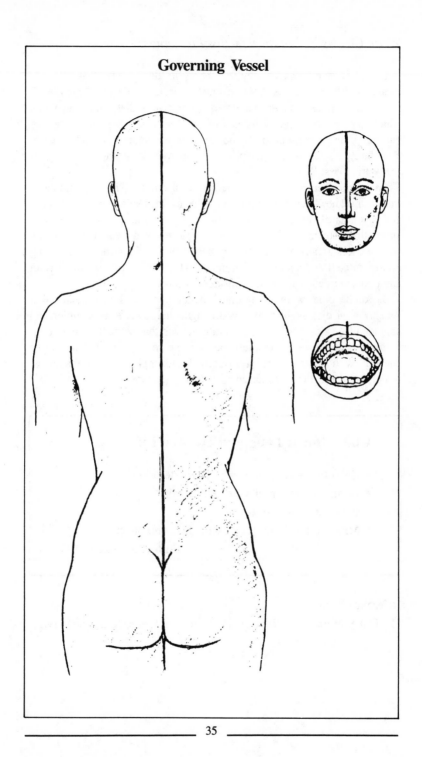

What Causes Imbalance in the Elements?

There are many reasons why the energy in the elements becomes imbalanced. When your health is adversely affected, your elements are effected. Sometimes you've made wrong choices in diet, choosing foods which deplete your energy instead of building it up. Sometimes you've pushed yourself to accomplish too much in too short a period of time. Your body creates unpleasant physical symptoms as a way of saying, "I really must rest!"

An excess of emotion can also deplete your energy. This is particularly true of unacknowledged emotion, a negative feeling that's become so habitual that you hardly realize that it's present. Early in life, you may have been taught that your needs do not count. If you received clear messages that you were less important than your brothers, you risked rejection by speaking up for yourself and acting "unfeminine." This kind of role scripting is an emotional burden that drains considerable energy.

As you become aware of any illness patterns in your life, you learn that symptoms of dis-ease can give you insight that leads to a healthier and happier life. Pain of any kind generally means that something is wrong. Learn to read the signals that tell you to take care of yourself. Familiarize yourself with Acupressure philosophy to recognize your imbalances. Acupressure self-therapy can correct these imbalances.

Guides for a Long and Healthy Life

- Keep the heart's emotions in moderation
- Limit the intake of food and drink
- Perform daily work
- Make it a rule to get enough rest and sleep

Li Shih-chen, circa 1593

Reference Note

1. Duke, Marc, *ACUPUNCTURE*, Harcourt, Brace, Jovanovich, 1972.

CHAPTER THREE
Premenstrual Syndrome

You may be one of the lucky women who never has a gynecological problem. Many women, however, have a vaginal or urinary tract infection that causes itching, pain and sexual problems at least once a year. Many more experience a distressing set of symptoms grouped together under the heading, Premenstrual Syndrome, popularly known as PMS. Sometimes these minor problems occur so frequently that they threaten the quality of your life. You may have tried a number of quick-fix remedies and found that they only work for a short time. As soon as you are stressed or over-tired, your symptoms return.

What is PMS?

PMS symptoms return month after month, causing fluid retention, nervousness and depression during the two weeks prior to your menstrual period. While only five percent of women require medical care, countless others experience varying degrees of physical and emotional disruption.[1] Your PMS symptoms may be mild ("My breasts get a little swollen, that's all.") or they may render you incapable of normal functioning for half a month.

PMS affects almost every major organ system in your body, and, according to Dr. Susan Lark, manifests up to 150 symptoms.[2] In addition to water retention and mood changes, women commonly report exhaustion, sweet cravings, outbreaks of acne, indigestion and muscular aching. Symptoms appear singly or in combination, with or without period pain. Some sources include period pain as a PMS symptom, but increasingly it's reported as a separate category.

PMS can begin with your first menstruation as early as age ten or appear later in your thirties. PMS usually increases in severity with increasing age and numbers of children. As menopause approaches, PMS symptoms are frequently aggravated. It is still unclear whether a woman in her forties with severe premenstrual anxiety is suffering from untreated PMS or menopausal symptoms.

If you suffer regularly from PMS, there is (with minor exception) immense relief once your menstrual flow begins. However, if you also have period pain and cramping, sometimes accompanied by nausea and vomiting, distress which may continue for a few days into your period.

Menstrual Cycle Events

- PROLIFERATIVE OR PRE-OVULATORY PHRASE. Every month when ovarian hormones (estrogen and progesterone) reach their lowest point, the hypothalamus in the brain stimulates the pituitary gland ("queen" gland that controls hormone action) to begin the menstrual cycle. The pituitary secretes FSH (follicle stimulating hormone) which in turn triggers an egg follicle in the ovary to mature and secrete estrogen. In the proliferative phase, the egg ripens, the lining of the uterus thickens and the cervix secretes infertile mucus. Stress can alter the timing of events during the proliferative phase.

- OVULATORY PHASE occurs around the fourteenth day of the cycle. Under the influence of LH (luteinizing hormone), an egg is released from the ovary, travels via the abdominal cavity to a fallopian tube and remains there for twelve to thirty-six hours. Basal body temperature changes before and after ovulation and the cervical mucus becomes fertile.

- LUTEAL or PREMENSTRUAL PHASE is dominated by the hormone, progesterone, secreted by the corpus luteum ("yellow body") at the site of the released egg. Progesterone prepares the body for pregnancy by changing metabolism. (In some women this causes PMS.) The breasts swell, the uterine lining continues to thicken and the cervical mucus changes its consistency. At the end of the luteal phase, prostaglandins (which cause the uterus to contract) become more active.

- MENSTRUAL PHASE consists of the familiar menstrual period. When the egg fails to become fertilized in the fallopian tube, the lining of the uterus disintegrates and ovarian hormone levels drop in the bloodstream. (Do not confuse "menstrual period" with "menstrual cycle.")

Note: The ovarian (female) hormones are chemical catalysts that affect your body in opposite ways. Estrogen lowers blood sugar; progesterone raises blood sugar. Estrogen synthesizes fat; progesterone breaks down fat. However, since hormone action is complementary as well as antagonistic, it over-simplifies matters to cite hormone imbalance alone as the cause of symptoms.

OVARIAN HORMONES, THE BREASTS, CERVIX AND ENDOMETRIUM IN YOUR MENSTRUAL CYCLE

		OVULATION	
THE BREASTS	NORMAL STATE		FLUID ACCUMULATION
THE OVARIES	FOLLICLE OVUM GROWTH OF FOLLICLE		CORPUS LUTEUM GROWTH AND DEGENERATION OF CORPUS LUTEUM
OVARIAN HORMONES IN THE BLOODSTREAM	ESTROGEN		ESTROGEN PROGESTERONE
THE CERVIX	DILATED CERVIX — ABUNDANT LIQUID MUCUS		CLOSED CERVIX — THICK, GELATINOUS MUCUS
THE ENDOMETRIUM	DE-STRUCTION / RECONSTRUCTION MENSTRUAL FLOW / 2 WEEKS AFTER MENSTRUATION		TRANSFORMATION 2 WEEKS BEFORE MENSTRUATION

©'86 A. Weston

What Causes Period Pain and PMS?

Experts differ over the causes of PMS, although it's now established that period pain is caused by excess prostaglandin F. (Prostaglandins are a group of fatty acids that stimulate the uterus and other involuntary muscles. There are nine groups of prostaglandins, each labelled with a letter of the alphabet.)

Period pain is aggravated by pelvic congestion caused by water and sodium retention. This type of monthly pain can also be increased when the reproductive organs are scarred from pelvic surgery, fibroid tumors or endometriosis. Scarring may also follow a bout of pelvic inflammatory dis-ease (PID) and/or use of an intrauterine birth control device.

An older theory suggests that menstrual pain is caused by the mechanical action of the cervix. During menstruation, the cervix stretches open (dilates) to release menstrual fluids. Dilation causes cramping. If the cervix is tight for some reason, dilation is prolonged and strenuous. After having a baby, which stretches the cervix, some women experience relief from PMS symptoms. However, this theory is confused by the fact that PMS symptoms can worsen with successive childbirths.

Until recently, PMS was thought to be a psychological condition that women used to get sympathy. Even today when PMS is defined as a dis-ease, you may still be told that you are to blame for your monthly problems. If you could only "pull yourself together" (resolve sexuality issues, calm your emotions, etc.), you would be free of troublesome symptoms. As a result of this attitude, you — like many other women — might deny yourself the care that you need.

This outdated viewpoint ignores the legitimate biological influences that contribute to PMS symptoms — the possibility of hormone imbalances, low blood sugar, lack of progesterone or sensitivity to progesterone. Poor health habits, notably lack of exercise and irregular diet heavy in sugar, salt and processed foods, worsens PMS.

American doctors have long treated a wide range of gynecological problems by "balancing" female hormones. However, Dr. Katharina Dalton, a British gynecologist, pioneered the use of natural progesterone (derived from yams and soybeans) specifically for PMS. Dalton claims that natural progesterone is free of many harmful side-effects associated with synthetic progesterone (otherwise known as "progestogen" or "progestin," the type of progesterone used in birth control pills and estrogen replacement therapy). In Dalton's experience, only natural progesterone works for PMS. Progesterone therapy is currently the gynecologist's treatment of choice for PMS, besides anti-inflammatory drugs (Nupril, Motrin) and tranquilizers.[3]

Pros and Cons of Progesterone Therapy

- Pros — Many women say progesterone therapy is the only treatment that works for premenstrual weight gain and hostility. Stephanie DeGraff Bender (see Recommended Reading), director of a PMS clinic in Colorado, combines progestrone therapy with counseling (to break the cycle of blame, guilt and denial) and stress management. Bender, who emphasizes the Dalton theory, says that progesterone side effects are minor.[4]

- Cons — It's difficult to accurately measure hormone levels that fluctuate by the hour in any given day. Furthermore, studies on alleged progesterone deficiency in the luteal phase show little difference in hormone levels between women with and without PMS.

Natural progesterone is inactivated by the liver when given by mouth; consequently, it must be injected or given by rectal suppository. (A new orally-given drug, progestoral, became available in 1986.) This expensive medication must be taken throughout the luteal phase, sometimes longer and in progressively larger doses, because effectiveness may dwindle with use. The drug has not yet been approved as a PMS treatment by the FDA (neither have birth control pills, diuretics or tranquilizers often prescribed for PMS). Dr. Michelle Harrison (see Recommended Reading) of the National Women's Health Network considers progesterone therapy to be a last resort because side-effects include skin rash, irregular bleeding, delayed period and burning at the injection site. Harrison claims patients respond well to diet and Vitamin B6 therapy.[5]

Dr. Guy Abraham proposed that PMS is caused by low blood sugar or hypoglycemia promoted by an inadequate diet and stress. This theory adopted by many holistic practitioners favors a non pharmacological approach. The hypoglycemia-reducing treatment concentrates on improving overall health by banning smoking and eliminating refined sugars, caffeine and red meat from the diet. Small meals (see "Quick Energy Foods") are eaten throughout the day to keep blood sugar levels high. Vitamin B6 is added along with regular exercise and relaxation techniques throughout the cycle.[6]

Dr. Penny Budoff believes PMS symptoms are caused by imbalanced prostaglandins. Imbalance causes the uterus to spasm painfully, and these intense contractions compress uterine blood vessels to increase period pain. A few of the prostaglandins also enter the bloodstream, causing dizziness when blood vessels constrict and dilate in rapid succession. Runaway prostaglandins may also slow down your circulation, producing exhaustion, chilling, pain and numbness in the hands and feet.[7]

PMS and Your Emotions

Premenstrual Syndrome is usually synonymous with mood swings that make a woman suffer from low self-esteem and seemingly inexplicable feelings of fear and anger. You may suddenly feel out of control when nothing seems to work. Your concentration is off and everything takes more of your energy. These symptoms have a way of disrupting your relationships. Gretchen says, "I used to break up with my boyfriend once every month, until I realized it was PMS picking the fights."

If PMS symptoms escalate beyond mere annoyance and become violent, you need to do something. It's unhealthy to have tantrums and/or eating or drinking binges two weeks of the month. While studies show that more anti-social acts do occur during the premenstrual period (implying that PMS makes women irrational), there is hope for PMS sufferers.[8] Your symptoms do not make you a weak, over emotional personality.

Do balance the amount of stress in your life and begin an Acupressure self-help program. Acupressure can calm you down when you feel upset or anxious.

Taking Charge of PMS Emotions

- The first step in taking charge of your PMS emotions is to log your daily moods along with any physical symptoms. Underline angry days in red in your diary and calendar. Plan rewarding experiences for difficult days. Give yourself an extra reward when you dissolve anger into action.

- Acknowledge that your PMS emotions run your life for a part of the month. Keep a daily diary and share any monthly mood changes with a close woman friend or counselor who encourages self-help. Talking about problems with an eye to action is therapeutic. Admitting that you need help is a sign of strength, not weakness.

- Record positive experiences in your luteal phase. Native Americans believed that women were most reflective and creative just prior to menstruation. Allow time for your artistic, musical or literary self to emerge and create during the premenstrual weeks. Encourage this process with affirmations and visualization (see Introduction).

- PMS self-care involves giving up coffee, sugar and other food addictions. These may be difficult to handle during the luteal phase. Seek help from a therapist, PMS support group, or other women who are working with PMS symptoms.

- Learn to love yourself, even on your angry days. Putting yourself down after a temper tantrum feeds into the problem. Guard against self-blame when you feel impatient, irritated or have treated others unfairly. Instead of agonizing, find a way to make amends and use the experience to plan a more effective way of coping with future "angry days."

A self-help approach of any sort automatically requires a willingness to learn, to change and release old patterns of thinking. One of the problems with the PMS dis-ease orientation is that it promotes dependency on prescribed and over-the-counter drugs. In contrast, self-care encourages you to take charge, even when you enlist help from supportive health professionals and/or counselors.

It is extremely important to draw a distinction between taking a responsible attitude and blaming yourself for failing to attain a physical ideal. If you have the habit of coming down too hard on yourself, you'll sabotage any postive action by creating more stress. Limit your put-downs and beware of judgmental health texts that blame PMS and other gynecological problems on a "negative attitude." Part of Acupressure self-care is boosting your own self-respect.

During your better weeks, create a support system of family, friends and colleagues. When your symptoms are at their worst, do not hesitate to ask for help.

Acknowledge the fact that you are vulnerable to PMS, even if your symptoms appear only for a few days each month. Although it's convenient to deny the illness side of life when you're not actively suffering, you will achieve better results when you come to terms with any tendency to illness.

Acupressure Self-Care

Self-care involves your whole person — emotions, spiritual outlook, relationships as well as diet and exercise habits. At any time during your menstruating years, you are more vulnerable to PMS if you're unhappy at home or on the job and your diet is poor. A fat-laden diet that frequently includes junk foods robs your body of the vitamins and minerals needed for healthy functioning. A fatty diet overworks your liver, and excess salt promotes fluid retention. Coffee and sugar, so much a part of the Western diet, deplete your body of the B-vitamins which keep your nervous system healthy and stabilize your emotions.

Acupressure self-care emphasizes the drug-free approach to PMS proposed by Abraham, Harrison, Lark and Dr. Marcia Storch. (Storch found that limiting salt and adding Vitamin B6 stopped water retention and resultant headaches eighty percent of the time.[9]) In addition to diet and behavior modification, this program adds the powerful balancing effect of Acupressure. Review the list of specific PMS symptoms that follow with their locations. Begin with your most troublesome symptoms. Acupressure is a powerful balancer, particularly when added to diet and behavior modification.

Positive Nutrition for PMS

- The amino acid, tryptophan, is a precursor of serotonin, a substance in the brain that with other key factors promotes endorphin secretion (see Chapter One for
a description of endorphins). Scientific studies show
tryptophan to be a safe, natural sedative and painkiller
that's now being used successfully for PMS symptoms.
You can buy tryptophan in a health food store.[10]

- Oil of primrose (also called Evening Primrose Oil) is
another nutrient effective against PMS and period pain.
As the richest source of gamma-linolenic acid (GLA),
it stimulates the production of prostaglandin E which
increases your ability to withstand stress. Oil of primrose and GLA are available in health food stores.

- Quick and easy vegetable stew provides nutrients to com-
bat PMS symptoms. Combine the following ingredients
in a covered pot and bring to a boil. Turn off heat but
leave pot on burner for one hour.

  3 cups chopped vegetables (carrots, celery, kale, spinach,
      cabbage, zucchini, sprouts, etc.)
  9 fresh tomatoes, liquified in a blender
  1 onion, diced
  1 teaspoon dried basil
  2 bay leaves
  4 cloves garlic (more or less, according to taste)
  2 cups water
  1/2 cup whole-grain pasta, if desired
  1/2 teaspoon tabasco or hot sauce, if desired
  1/2 to 3/4 cup tofu, finely chopped

Contingency Plan for PMS

- Create a support system. Make partners, housemates, and colleagues aware of the situation and enlist their help in planning and organizing difficult days.

- Make one improvement in your eating habits starting on day one of your menstrual cycle. Reinforce this change by logging it in your daily diary.

- If you are discouraged because PMS is severe month after month, get outside help by scheduling massage and Acupressure treatments during your most difficult week. Allow yourself time to develop Acupressure skills by pressing three points that relieve your most troublesome symptoms every day. As you gain better control over your emotions, you'll be able to take over with self-treatment.

- Plan domestic tasks ahead of time. For example, maintain a list of staple foods and household products, including foods which can be prepared quickly and easily. Have these in the house at all times.

- Plan professional tasks ahead of time. For example schedule important conferences and decisions during the proliferative phase of your cycle whenever possible.

- Meet with a PMS group during your luteal phase. If none is available and your emotions seem out of hand, see a holistic counselor immediately.

Acupressure Points for Emotional Symptoms of PMS

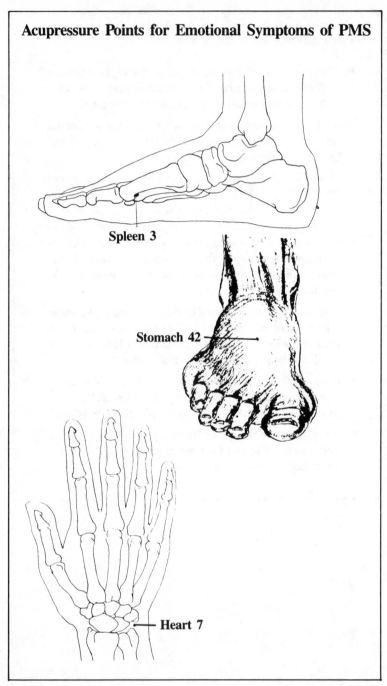

Spleen 3

Stomach 42

Heart 7

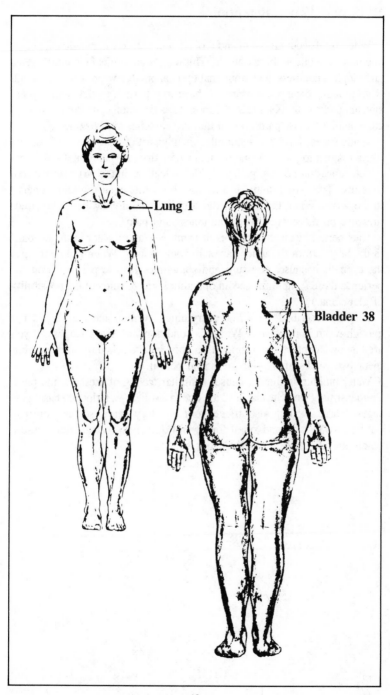

Lung 1

Bladder 38

PMS and Water Retention

When fluid accumulates in and around your cells during the luteal phase, you may gain one to three pounds. This causes abdominal bloating, breast and nipple tenderness, and emotional upset about the weight gain. Although PMS bloating disappears when you have your period, anxiety and depression about the extra pounds is common. Less common complaints are muscular aching, wrist pain and numbness, earache, and dizziness.

While excess fluid can accumulate in any part of your body, it is drawn like a magnet to joints. Some women suffer from carpal tunnel syndrome which causes numbness, pain and prickly feelings in the wrist from nerve pressure. The carpal tunnel is a narrow, bony tunnel surrounding a nerve in the wrist. When the cells of the carpal tunnel are swollen with fluid, pressure on the nerve causes numbness and pain.

Your period headaches can result from buildup of water in the eyeball, in the labyrinth of the inner ear or in your sinuses. When fluid engorges the eyeball, it causes pressure and sometimes intense pain. (If you experience these symptoms, see an opthalmologist to rule out the possibility of glaucoma.)

Barbara described, "It's like everything's swollen and there's just not enough room in my head." With this condition, eye size changes. (If you are having a contact lens fitting, it's a good idea to schedule your appointment two weeks after your menstrual period.)

Water buildup in the ear causes a similar feeling of pressure and pain. Premenstrual "sinus headaches" are due to swollen, waterlogged nasal passages. Nasal swelling also affects your olfactory nerve, so that you may not be able to taste and smell for several days each month. Acupressure points are effective in clearing your sinuses.

Acupressure Points for Water Retention Symptoms

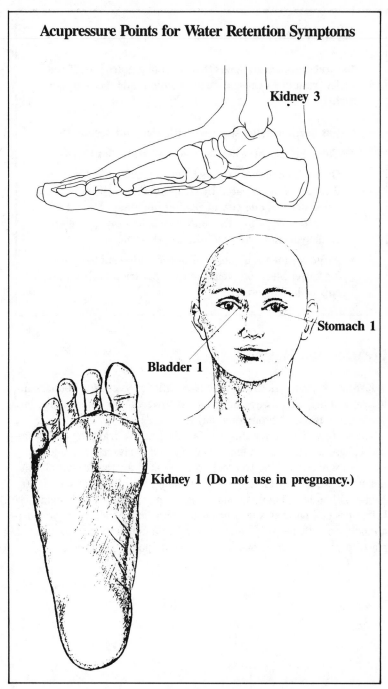

Kidney 3

Stomach 1

Bladder 1

Kidney 1 (Do not use in pregnancy.)

Natural Diuretics

Natural diuretics are foods that stimulate water loss. If you suffer from PMS-caused water retention, add them to your diet.

- Eat garlic raw or steamed with rice and vegetables.
- Cabbage can be eaten in coleslaw, soups and stews.
- Drink three to four cups per day of parsley tea, a strong diuretic. It is prepared by steeping one teaspoon of the dried herb in one cup of boiling hot water. Do not exceed four cups per day and watch for any symptoms of dehydration, dry mouth, for example.
- Anise seed tea is a gentler diuretic with a subtle, pleasing taste. Steep one teaspoon of the dried herb in one cup of boiling water.

Premenstrual Fatigue

Just before your period, you may have little or no energy. You lack initiative and the will to carry out plans. If it weren't for coffee and sugar, you'd never make it through the day.

There are biological reasons for your fatigue. Waterlogging during the luteal phase causes a shift in mineral action. Sodium is retained while potassium is excreted, making you feel tired, weak and irritable. Restore this mineral imbalance by limiting (or eliminating) your intake of salty foods, including hot dogs, bouillion and potato chips. Then add potassium-rich kelp, apricots, peaches and bananas to your diet. Acupressure provides a quick, no-caffeine pick-me-up. Instead of a coffee break, find a quiet place to relax and press one or more of the points given in Chart 3.

Acupressure Points for Premenstrual Fatigue

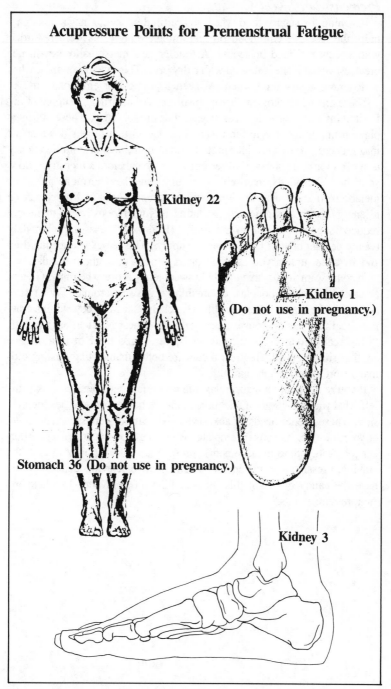

Kidney 22

Kidney 1
(Do not use in pregnancy.)

Stomach 36 (Do not use in pregnancy.)

Kidney 3

Premenstrual Sweet Craving

Reaching for sugary food when you're tired or feeling negative is partially the result of childhood programming. Many of us were rewarded with sweets for good behavior. (A toddler gets marshmallows with her breakfast cereal if she wakes up with a dry bed.) This kind of reward teaches us to crave sugary food when we need a physical or emotional lift.

There are also biological factors involved. An insufficient supply of the B-vitamins and magnesium can trigger a desire for sugar. These nutrients play an important role in the metabolic process that breaks down sugar into glucose. Your body interprets B-vitamin and magnesium deficiency as a need for more sugar. Furthermore, the week before a menstrual flow, your body responds intensely to insulin (the key hormone in sugar metabolism) and leaves the bloodstream to enter cells and be converted to energy. With less glucose circulating in your bloodstream, there is a reduced supply available to the brain. (Brain work uses approximately twenty percent of your body's energy supply.) This leaves you feeling tired and irritable, unless you eat high energy foods throughout the day.

In some women, the urge to nibble sweet foods is overwhelming. Gretchen says, "If there's chocolate or anything else sweet around, I don't have any say in the matter." Yet you, like Gretchen, can work beyond this craving. Begin by having your quick energy food nearby. Then ask youself, "Am I really hungry?" If the answer is,"yes," eat a piece of fruit or have another snack. Small, frequent meals are better than fasting (fasting ultimately promotes weight gain).

If you're not really hungry, relax and take a few deep breaths. Ask yourself what you really want. Quiet time alone? A litle excitement, less depression? These deeper needs, if acknowledged, call for some rearrangement of your lifestyle. As you contemplate the changes you might make (a different job, better time management), press Acupressure points to ease the craving. Pressing a point can also be an effective delaying tactic! "I won't have the candy bar right this minute, I'll wait until after I've held my Acupressure points."

Quick Energy Foods

If you are prone to fatigue, raise your blood sugar level by eating high energy "mini-meals." Avoid coffee, sugar or gum for a quick lift, because you'll have an energy letdown a few hours later. Quick energy foods provide a natural energy boost. Carry them in your purse, briefcase or bookbag.

Apple
Apricot
Banana
Pear
Grapes
Whole-wheat crackers
Whole-grain muffins or biscuits
Peeled broccoli stalks
Steamed green beans
Unsalted nuts or dried soybeans

Herbal teas also provide quick energy. Mullein tea is an old remedy for exhaustion, sweet craving and irritability. Use one teaspoon to one cup boiling water. Burdock root tea is said to strengthen the blood and increase energy. Steep one teaspoon of ground burdock in one cup of boiling water. You can drink up to two cups per day.

Acupressure Points for Premenstrual Sweet Craving.

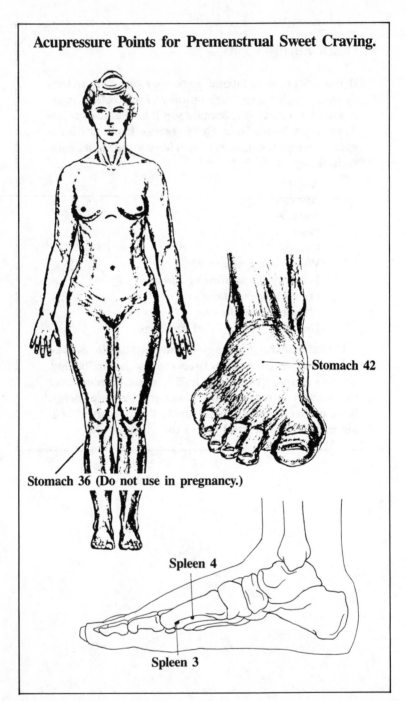

Stomach 42

Stomach 36 (Do not use in pregnancy.)

Spleen 4

Spleen 3

Period Pain and Indigestion

Menstrual cramps range from minor twinges to severe, disabling pain. Since cramps are nothing more than uterine spasms, your self-treatment program should focus on relaxation. Tense muscles in the solar plexus and abdomen aggravate the period pain and indigestion. Barbara was able to minimize monthly pain by pressing Acupressure points twice a day (before she got out of bed in the morning and during her lunch hour). If she practiced deep breathing while pressing the points, she got better results. Gretchen used natural muscle relaxants as supplements to the Acupressure points in Chart 5. When her cramps were intense, she took 1000 mg. of calcium and magnesium in combination with warm milk. Mary found that sex relaxed her enough to take away her period pain.

Period pain is aggravated by acid indigestion or constipation. For relief, supplement the Acupressure points in Chart 5 by chewing a handful of ripe grapes (grapes have a laxative effect). Do use Acupressure. You will get better results if you are familiar with points before your pain begins.

If you experience pelvic pain throughout the month, consider other causes than PMS. Pelvic pain can be the result of trauma and simple tension or it can be an indicator of a more serious problem that requires medical help. Persistent pelvic pain is a symptom of pelvic inflammatory dis-ease, endometriosis, cystitis and other illnesses. Consult a gynecologist promptly. Painful intercourse may also result from use of a diaphragm (improperly fitted) or inserted incorrectly.

Acupressure Points for Period Pain and Indigestion

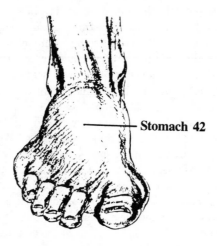

Stomach 42

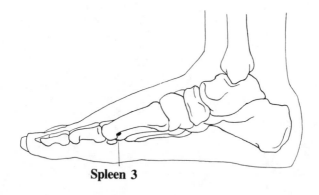

Spleen 3

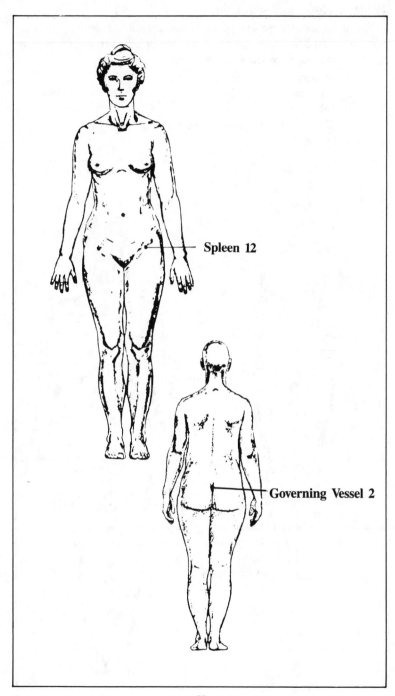

Spleen 12

Governing Vessel 2

Point Series for Period Pain

This point series to relieve period pain takes ten minutes of your time. For maximum benefit, hold the points in the order given and do not hurry. After the sequence, relax a few minutes.

1. Bladder 47.
2. Conception Vessel 4.
3. Spleen 6.
   (Do not use this point in pregnancy.)
4. Spleen 13.

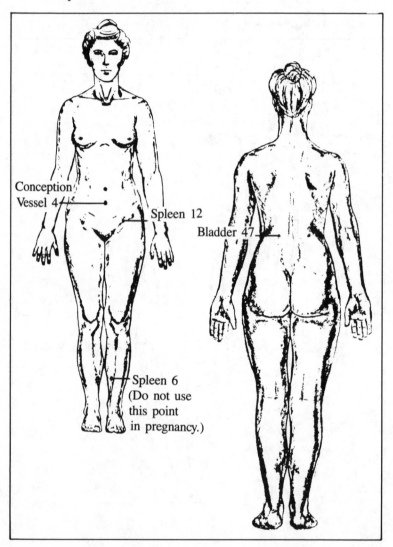

PMS and Sex

Lovemaking may be a pleasant form of stress reduction during your luteal phase. However, PMS moods can cause relationship problems which interfere with sex. If you're having resentful feelings, it's difficult to become aroused and lubricate for comfortable intercourse. The result can be dyspareunia (painful intercourse) or vaginismus (vaginal tightening that makes penetration painful or impossible), your body's method of conscientious objection.

Chronic pelvic tension makes it difficult to receive your lover without pain. Have a gynecologist rule out a medical problems like endometriosis or a torn uterine ligament, resulting from childbirth. Pelvic tightness and pain can also be the residue of a traumatic sexual experience, rather than dis-ease or stress. If you've been the victim of sexual violence, you may well require a period of celibacy and supportive counseling from an experienced woman psychotherapist.

For less serious problems, added lubrication in the form of any vegetable oil at room temperature can make coitus easier. (Asian medical practitioners associate a lack of vaginal fluid with imbalanced kidneys, seen as the center of sexual energy. Pressing Acupressure points tonifies the kidneys and stimulates vaginal secretions.) Orgasm is one of the best cures for pelvic tension, cramps and period pain (if unrelated to dis-ease). Like a good night's sleep, sex with a loving partner is one of life's great restorers.

If you are tight all over from PMS-related tension, it will be difficult for you to enjoy lovemaking. This is remedied by taking the time to relax with your partner before making love. Listen to music, talk quietly and press Acupressure points on each other. You may also be helped by a lengthier, more sophisticated approach to sex that includes innovative foreplay.

Acupressure Points to Relieve Pelvic Tension

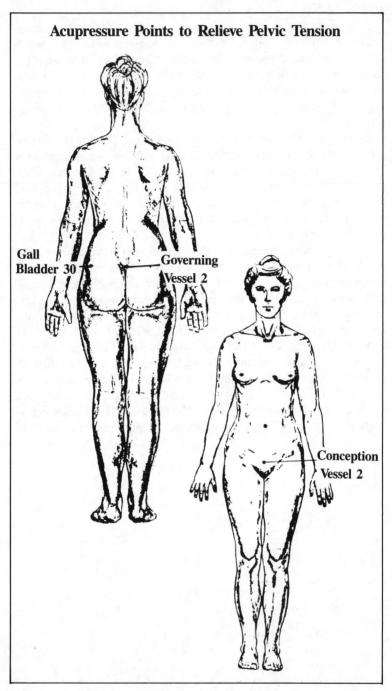

Gall
Bladder 30

Governing
Vessel 2

Conception
Vessel 2

Acupressure Points for Insufficient Vaginal Lubrication

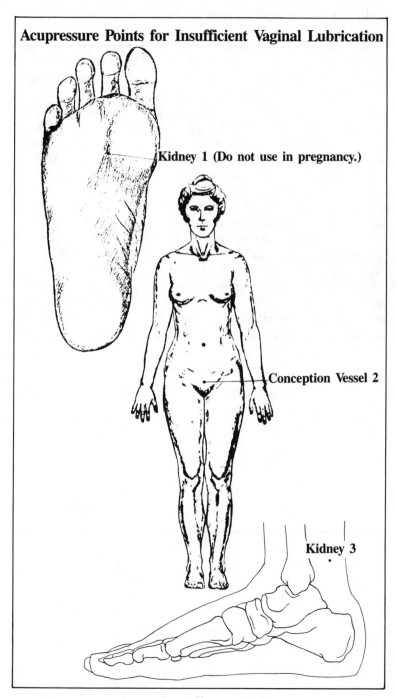

Kidney 1 (Do not use in pregnancy.)

Conception Vessel 2

Kidney 3

PMS Backache and Muscular Pain

Low back pain is a premenstrual problem for many women. A dull ache spreads from your waist down through the hips and just stays there for days at a time. Pain in this area is a clear indicator of deficient kidney energy. Rubbing the kidneys relieves low back tension.

Premenstrual backache is sometimes the result of water accumulation in the discs between the vertebrae. As noted above, water can build up in any of your tissues, including muscular tissue, causing overall achiness and sensitivity. If you bump yourself, the bruise is twice as painful as usual. You may also feel like you cannot bear to move or be touched. Fluid buildup is a sign of deficient kidney energy.

Supplement the Acupressure points in Chart 8 with exercise. Regular exercise (not just pushing yourself to swim or run when you feel tense and achy) prevents fluid buildup in the muscles and organs. A program of stretching balanced with bicycling, running or swimming improves your stamina and keeps your joints flexible.

If you haven't exercised recently, it's a good idea to start with walking. Add a twenty-minute walk to your daily routine by getting off the bus a few stops early or walking to the grocery store instead of taking the car. Remember to build stamina slowly, and remind yourself that "good" equals "a little better than last week."

Acupressure Points for Backache and Muscular Pain

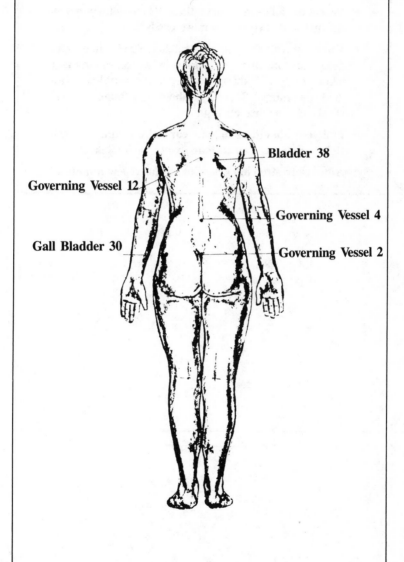

Bladder 38

Governing Vessel 12

Governing Vessel 4

Gall Bladder 30

Governing Vessel 2

Stretches

- First, take a few moments to sit or lie quietly while you relax your breathing.

- Repeat the following affirmations: "I feel calm and confident" and "My joints move easily."

- Warm up with slow, gentle stretches. Stretch like a cat, extending your arms and legs as far as you can manage comfortably. (If you stretch regularly, you'll soon extend your range.) Be realistic about your limitations. Go slowly if you have an injury.

- Pull your shoulders to your ears. Press chin to chest. Relax. Extend head to touch your back. Relax.

- After your stretching, lie quietly for a few minutes.

A Guide for Stretching

WATER WHEEL

FLAPPING WINGS

CROSS STRETCH

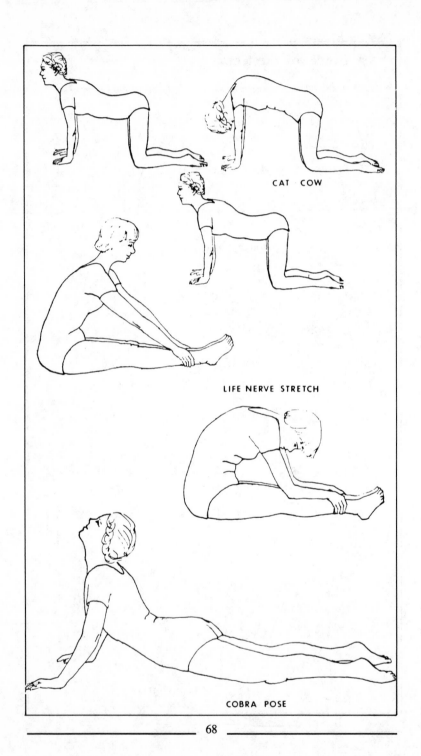

CAT COW

LIFE NERVE STRETCH

COBRA POSE

PMS and Acne

Acne and oily hair signal "I'm premenstrual" to many women. Curiously, this is caused by a higher level of male hormones (androgens) in your body. When your adrenal glands rev up during the luteal phase, they activate oil glands in your skin. Use a balanced diet with a minimum of sugar, fat and chemical additives to prevent premenstrual acne. (Substitute cold chicken for the peanut butter in your daily sandwich. Cut fats and oil intake by half.) Shampoo hair and wash skin frequently with non-allergenic soaps designed for oily complexions. By stimulating circulation, Acupressure points can help to prevent oil from clogging your complexion.

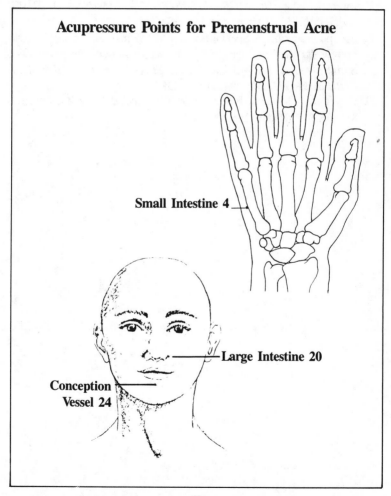

Acupressure Points for Premenstrual Acne

Small Intestine 4

Large Intestine 20

Conception Vessel 24

Reference Notes
1. Lark, Susan, *DR. SUSAN LARK'S PREMENSTRUAL SELF-HELP SYNDROME*, Forman Publishing Co., 1984.
2. Ibid.
3. Dalton, Katharina, *THE PREMENSTRUAL SYNDROME AND PROGESTERONE THERAPY*, second edition, Year Book Medical Publishers, Inc., Chicago, 1984.
4. Bender, Stephanie DeGraff et al., *PMS, A POSITIVE PROGRAM TO GAIN CONTROL*, The Body Press, Tucson, AZ, 1986.
5. Harrison, Michelle, *SELF-HELP FOR PREMENSTRUAL SYNDROME*, Random House, rev. 1982.
6. Abraham, Guy, *PREMENSTRUAL BLUES*, Porter and Griffin, 1982.
7. Budoff, Penny, *NO MORE MENSTRUAL CRAMPS AND OTHER GOOD NEWS*, Viking-Penguin, 1982.
8. Second Opinion, "A Special Issue on Premenstrual Tension," *Coalition for the Medical Rights of Women*, San Francisco, September 1983.
9. Storch, Marcia, *HOW TO RELIEVE CRAMPS AND OTHER MENSTRUAL PROBLEMS*, Workman, 1983.
10. Prevention Magazine Editors, *UNDERSTANDING VITAMINS AND MINERALS*, Rodale Press, 1984.

CHAPTER FOUR
Pregnancy, Birth and Nursing

Preconception Period Self-Help Program

Holistic prenatal care begins with your decision to conceive a child. It is important to start preparing yourself for pregnancy as soon as you decide you want children, even if you're going to wait a few years. Pregnancy, birth and nursing are normal, natural experiences, but they make great demands upon your body and spirit. The ease of your pregnancy and birth and the well being of your baby depend greatly upon your general health. If you are healthy and energetic before you conceive, you'll have, in most cases, a more positive birth outcome.

The preconception period is an optimal time to use Acupressure self-treatment. After taking stock of your health habits, including your diet and exercise program, you can start pressing Acupressure points to maximize your reproductive energies.

Herbs to Avoid When You are Pregnant or Nursing a Baby

The herbs listed below are too strong to use during pregnancy. As soon as you decide to become pregnant, eliminate them from your diet.

Golden seal
Valerian
Ginger
Cotton root
Motherwort
Tansy
Vervain
Couchgrass
Squawgrass or cohosh
Pennyroyal
Sage
Rue
Ginseng
St. John's Wort

Focus upon building up the kidneys, to increase the likelihood of a successful pregnancy. Give yourself a kidney rub daily and add black beans (a kidney builder) to your diet.

Supplement your Acupressure program by taking a good look at your eating habits. Once you are pregnant, you will literally be eating for two. What you give to your body, you give to your developing baby. It is never too soon to develop better eating patterns to nurture the two of you.

Black Bean Tonic

Black beans are a traditional remedy for building up the kidneys. Eat them daily during the preconception period. Soak the dry beans overnight in plenty of water. Next day, discard the water and rinse the beans in a colander. Boil beans until they are soft enough to chew (thirty to forty-five minutes). Drain beans and store in your refrigerator. Eat two to three tablespoons per day.

Kidney Rub

During the preconception period, give yourself a kidney rub each day to energize your kidneys. Make your hands into loose fists and put them behind your back at the level of your waist. Rub vigorously in an up-and-down motion 100 times. It feels good to do this in the shower with a stream of water running down your back.

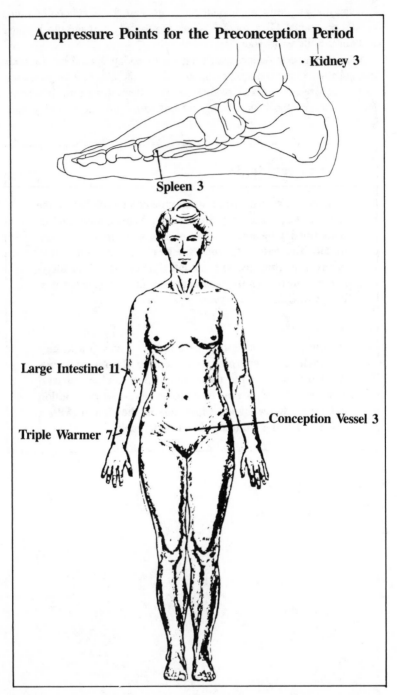

Acupressure Points for the Preconception Period

· Kidney 3

Spleen 3

Large Intestine 11

Triple Warmer 7

Conception Vessel 3

Pregnancy

The conception and growth of a new human being is the most joyful of mysteries. Now that you are pregnant, your body is hard at work all of the time. Embryonic cells differentiate rapidly into the baby's limbs, eyes and brain. At six weeks, your baby has a beating heart and nerves that fire messages all over his/her body. As he/she continues to develop, you grow an entirely new organ, which serves as a nutrient and oxygen exchange. This blood-rich placenta is attached to the umbilical cord where your blood vessels are entwined with the baby's. The foods you eat every day become the nutrients carried along this pathway.

As a pregnant and lactating woman, you require more calories (dieting is hazardous to you and your baby) and protein in your diet. Your balanced diet should consist of vitamins, minerals, complex carbohydrates (whole grains) and body-building protein. (See Recommended Readings.) High-grade protein is the foundation of fetal development, particularly brain growth. Protein also supports the blood-building process that almost doubles throughout pregnancy. In pregnancy, this extra blood circulates through your body to supply your added metabolic needs and nourish your baby via the placental exchange.

As your uterus enlarges, it presses your bladder, causing frequent urination. The increased hormone output activates your sweat and oil glands and stimulate the output of cervical mucus.

Cynthia said, "I keep thinking that my body will never be the same again." Acupressure can relieve nausea and backache. There are points for birthing, postpartum pain and nursing problems. Throughout your pregnancy, you can utilize Acupressure to calm and center your emotions and provide relief from uncomfortable symptoms.

Dietary Adjustments Make the Difference

Sarah wanted desperately to have a baby. Although she used Acupressure faithfully for two years to conceive, she was unsuccessful until she stopped using caffeine and sugar.

Stimulants like coffee, black tea and colas sabotage your Acupressure self-treatment program, because caffeine and white sugar injure the kidneys. Caffeine elevates the level of serum uric acid, making it difficult for the kidneys to function properly. White sugar overstimulates the kidneys.

It's not easy to cut out caffeine, when coffee-drinking has been a long-time satisfaction. Sarah avoided typical withdrawal symptoms by reducing coffee intake by a half-cup per day. She substituted Yogi Tea, nourishing cups of broth and heated apple juice to have something warm to hold in her hands. Soon, she scarcely missed her morning wake-up coffee and afternoon pick-up.

Acupressure Points to Avoid During Pregnancy

Do not use these points after your decision to become pregnant. They are traditionally forbidden for expectant mothers.

Small Intestine 7	Triple Warmer 4
Small Intestine 10	Triple Warmer 10
Kidney 1	Gall Bladder 2
Kidney 2	Gall Bladder 9
Kidney 4	Gall Bladder 34
Kidney 7	Pericardium 8
Lung 7	Pericardium 6
Lung 11	Large Intestine 2
Stomach 4	Large Intestine 4
Stomach 36	Large Intestine 10
Stomach 4	Spleen 1
Stomach 36	Spleen 2
Stomach 45	Spleen 6

YOUR FIRST TRIMESTER

The first trimester is a time of body change and emotional ambivalence. The most common complaints are nausea, fatigue and breast tenderness.

Nausea, Vomiting and Indigestion

Prenatal nausea or morning sickness is one of the most unpleasant side-effects of early pregnancy. Not only is it annoying to get sick in the kitchen and car (cooking odors and car exhaust are particularly offensive), but severe nausea can depress and almost disable a previously healthy woman.

Acupressure is effective for nausea and vomiting but you will have to make dietary and lifestyle adjustments to have the best results. Since nausea usually occurs with an empty stomach, have a protein snack at bedtime and keep whole grain crackers (soda crackers are a poor quality food) by your bedside to eat before you arise in the morning. Rice cakes, grapes and papaya are also well tolerated. Lie in bed while you nibble and use this time to press Acupressure points and practice relaxation. Chew your food thoroughly to avoid further discomfort, and ask your partner to bring you a cup of herbal tea (or keep a thermos handy). Spearmint, peppermint and raspberry leaf tea are classic herbal remedies for prenatal nausea.

During the day, eat small but nutritious meals to relieve nausea and heartburn. Diet modification requires planning. Mary was a teacher who suffered from morning sickness. In class, she ate grapes every hour. At 10:00, she took 20 minutes to press points and suck on a mint tea ice cube.

It's estimated that two-thirds of all pregnant women experience some first trimester nausea. The latest theory correlates nausea with higher-than-usual amounts of the hormone, chorionic gonadotrophin. But not everyone with this ailment is nauseated in the morning. Kathleen had afternoon sickness and was weak and queasy by 3:00 PM.

It took some strategizing — and Acupressure — for Kathleen to stay on the job. Previously, she'd skipped breakfast and had a heavy lunch as the main meal of the day. Her Acupressurist recommended a more substantial breakfast, a light but nourishing lunch and fruit or crackers with herb tea in mid-afternoon. With each meal she began to press Acupressure points, a successful plan that allowed her to attend afternoon board meetings.

Acupressure Points for Prenatal Nausea and Indigestion

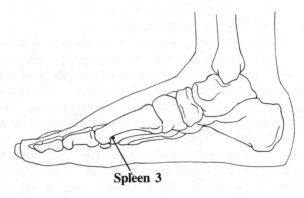

Spleen 3

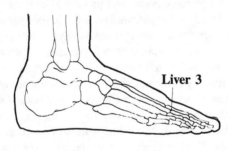

Liver 3

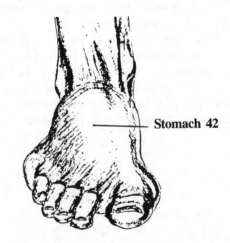

Stomach 42

Prenatal Fatigue

Most women complain about prenatal fatigue in the first and third trimesters. Feeling tired is a particular problem for women who do not acknowledge the physical and emotional demands of pregnancy. You have every right to adjust your life so that you can sleep or rest whenever you feel like it. Accordingly, you may have to let other important projects go.

Susan, a nurse on a cancer ward and her husband, Michael, a firefighter, sought help because they were too tired and overextended to enjoy either the pregnancy or their four-year-old daughter. Upon advice, they started trading massage and Acupressure and Susan reduced her work hours. This extra rest renewed her stamina and made her more efficient at the hospital. Susan declared, "I needed someone to tell me that it was okay to cut down. Now I feel so special, being pregnant."

While your body works double time in first trimester, it's understandable that you'll have less energy than usual. During mid-pregnancy, you may experience a characteristic surge of energy. Do not overdo at this phase or you'll find yourself drained for the more taxing third trimester. Help yourself along by scheduling rest periods during the day, even if you work outside of your home. Find a way to prop up your feet and relax — then deepen that relaxation — for fifteen minutes three times a day. These rest periods offer opportunities to use Acupressure. and to connect with your baby using affirmations and visualization (see Chapter One). Say to yourself, "My baby and I are resting." "We'll be ready and rested when labor begins." Form a clear mental image of yourself holding a healthy, smiling infant.

Acupressure Points for Prenatal Fatigue

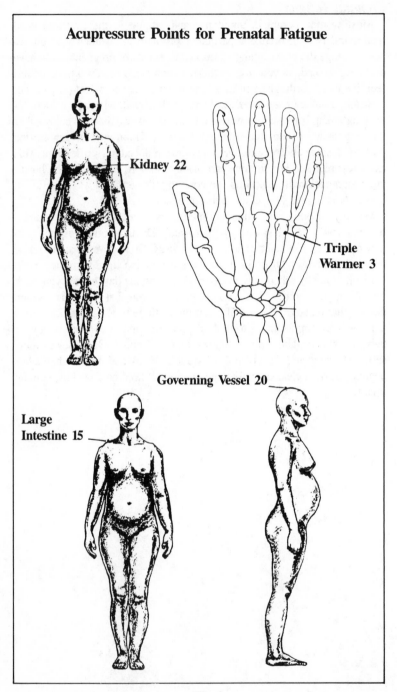

Kidney 22

Triple Warmer 3

Governing Vessel 20

Large Intestine 15

Breast Tenderness

By the twelfth week of pregnancy, your nipples are darker and veins are prominent on the surface of your breasts. At the sixteenth week, the areola around the nipples becomes mottled. (All of these changes are to be expected. Of course, any extreme discomfort or unusual discharge should be reported to your obstetrical caregiver.)

Enlarged and tender breasts are usually the first sign of pregnancy. As milk ducts elaborate to prepare for lactation, you may notice a prickly, tingling feeling that can be bothersome in the first two months. For relief, apply gentle pressure to Acupressure points on your chest, using your palms instead of fingertip pressure. Palming the points on sensitive areas can be as effective as direct pressure.

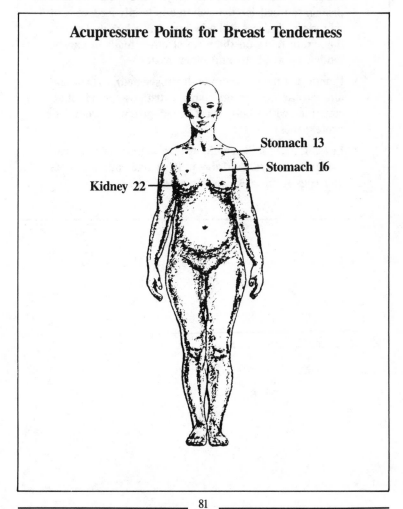

Acupressure Points for Breast Tenderness

Stomach 13

Stomach 16

Kidney 22

Convenient, Inexpensive Protein Foods

Although Americans often consume an over-supply of protein, pregnant women must increase their protein stores to support an expanded blood volume. Protein is also essential for the formation of brain cells in your developing baby. Add these convenient, inexpensive protein sources to your diet.

- Tofu is available in the produce section of most supermarkets. Manufactured from soybeans, it is a complete protein source, rich in calcium and totally fat-free. Cut tofu in small pieces and add it to your salads and soups. Since tofu takes on the taste of other foods, it can be hidden in spaghetti and other pastas.

- Peanut (use the natural, non-hydrogenated), cashew and almond butters are delicious, nutritious spreads that, combined with whole wheat bread, give you a complete protein meal.

- Low-fat, dried milk should be used in place of chemical-loaded creamers. Add dry milk to fruit juices, sauces and eggs to increase your protein intake.

YOUR SECOND TRIMESTER

Most women feel more energetic and optimistic in second trimester. Common discomforts include nasal congestion, heartburn, and constipation.

Nasal Congestion

Nasal congestion and plugged ear can be a problem. Even in the absence of infection, you may suffer from nasal congestion in the second trimester, because your mucous membranes are sensitive to the extra hormones produced in pregnancy. If you have sinus trouble or are miserable with a cold, you can't reach for something in the medicine chest. Drugs like antihistamines, decongestants and painkillers are taboo in pregnancy.

There are Acupressure points to clear your nasal passages and ears and relieve painful sinus pressure. If you suffer from respiratory problems of any kind, use these points early in the morning when you are likely to have the most discomfort. Mary, who was miserable with "sinus," started her day by pressing points in the shower.

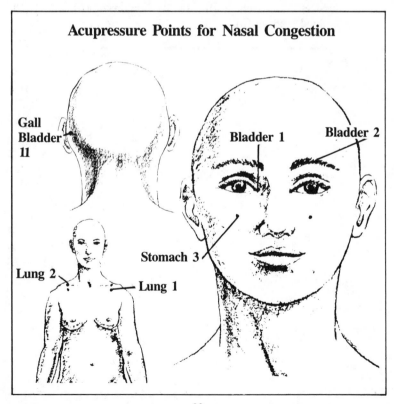

Acupressure Points for Nasal Congestion

Gall Bladder 11

Bladder 1

Bladder 2

Stomach 3

Lung 2

Lung 1

Natural Cold Remedies

Every pregnant and nursing woman should be strongly discouraged from using over-the-counter cold preparations. If distressing cold symptoms occur, you can substitute Acupressure and other traditional remedies.

- Boneset tea is made by steeping one teaspoon of the herb in one cup of boiling water for half an hour. Drink one tablespoon of this tea at a time, three to six times per day.

- Cayenne is used to build up resistance at the onset of a cold. Steep one teaspoon of cayenne pepper in one cup of boiling water. Drink one cup per day, a mouthful at a time throughout the day.

- Rest is a tried and true cold remedy. You may be able to sleep away your sniffles before they become a full-fledged cold or flu.

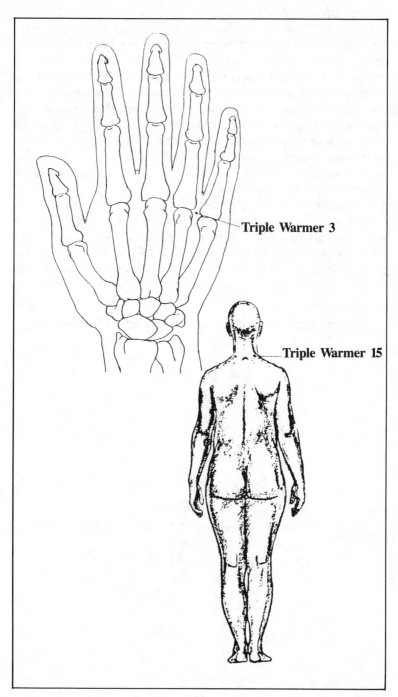

Triple Warmer 3

Triple Warmer 15

Heartburn and Constipation

Nausea and fatigue usually disappear in the second trimester. However, you may notice an unpleasant burning sensation in the area of your throat or chest after a full meal. "Heartburn," as this condition is called, is a misnomer. Actually, when your stomach is distended with food and pressed by the large uterus, gastric fluid bubbles upward because the valve between your esophagus (food pipe) and stomach is less efficient in pregnancy.

Usually antacids are recommended for heartburn. Instead, try papaya (fruit, juice or tablet) which contains digestive enzymes, yogurt if it's a lactobacillus culture and whole grains to digest your food better. Eating small amounts of food four to six times a day is an old remedy. If you do have heartburn, press Acupressure points and cross your arms behind your head for awhile. Do press points every day for prevention.

Constipation is common in pregnancy for two reasons. Your digestive organs are crowded and supplemental iron and calcium are binding. For relief, you need to exercise daily and eat laxative foods. Yogurt, bran, wheat germ and an abundance of fresh fruits and vegetables will make a difference.

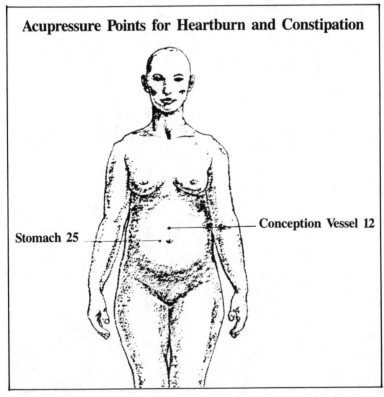

Acupressure Points for Heartburn and Constipation

Conception Vessel 12

Stomach 25

Natural Headache Remedies

During pregnancy, be wary of using any kind of medication — prescription, over-the-counter or "recreational" drugs. Acupressure is a safe, natural substitute for your aspirin or Tylenol. Add a gentle scalp massage to increase circulation and release tension in the muscles of your head and neck. Herbal remedies can provide relief from discomfort.

- Nettle tea is made by steeping three tablespoons of the herb in one cup of boiling water for ten minutes.

- Yerba Santa tea is made by steeping one teaspoon of the herb in one cup of boiling water for ten minutes.

Acupressure Points for Headache Relief

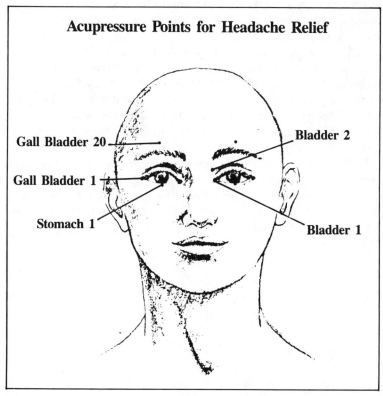

Gall Bladder 20

Gall Bladder 1

Stomach 1

Bladder 2

Bladder 1

YOUR THIRD TRIMESTER

It's a challenge to stay comfortable in the third trimester. The most common complaints are backache, stitch in the side, swollen hands and feet, carpal tunnel syndrome and shortness of breath. If you are overdue, it's easy to become discouraged and depressed.

Backache and Muscular Tension

Prenatal weight gain redistributes the pounds that you carry, altering your center of gravity. Your heavy uterus is supported by broad ligaments attached to your back. Unless you have very strong abdominal muscles, you're literally carrying your baby with your back muscles. If these muscles are weak, you're at high risk for developing chronic back problems. Under the best circumstances, you'll have a tendency to lean backwards in the third trimester.

Acupressure, regular exercise and good body mechanics will spare your over-worked back. Learn how to move your body economically when you get out of bed or climb in and out of the car. Practice the positive pregnancy stance early in pregnancy to make it a habit by the third trimester. Avoid situps and use a pillow between the curve of your lower back and the chair or carseat.

Be sure that any fitness program you attend in the third trimester meets the special needs of the pregnant woman. Fast walking (work up to at least a mile) and swimming will also keep your muscles relaxed and flexible. Yoga or any stretching and long, slow breathing will help you slough off tensions. Special childbearing exercises include the pelvic tilt and the Kegel, each practiced eighty times per day. Low-impact aerobics appear safe if you are physically fit.

If you experience any muscle strain or backache, alternate hot and cold compresses to the area. Keep a heating pad or hot washcloth on the muscle for five minutes (do not burn yourself) and replace it with an ice pack or for another five minutes. Repeat, adding Acupressure for maximum relief.

Grounding Yourself with the Positive Pregnancy Stance

- Plant your feet eight inches wider apart than usual and point feet straight ahead to improve balance and stability.

- Flex your knees. Notice how you carry your weight differently. (Locked knees cause knee problems, sway-back and tension in the thighs). Learn to keep your knees flexible to lower the chances of injury and reduce tension buildup in the lower back.

- Pull your shoulders back slightly and lift your breast-bone. This reduces tension in the chest and upper back. Observe how it's easier to breathe.

- Use this stance throughout the day, ideally in the early months, so the posture comes naturally in the third trimester.

- With a first baby, you'll "lighten" (baby drops deeper into pelvis) two to six weeks before birthing. You may unconsciously lose the positive pregnancy stance. Deliberately counteract that tendency by assuming the pregnancy stance.

Acupressure Points for Backache and Muscular Stiffness

Triple Warmer 15

Bladder 38

Bladder 47

Governing Vessel 4

Gall Bladder 30

Governing Vessel 2

Bladder 42

Stitch in the Side

Stitch in the side is really a round ligament spasm that occurs when you laugh, sneeze or move about suddenly. For instant relief, breathe in and stretch your arm upward on the affected side. Hold the stretch as long as you can, breathing deeply. If you still have pain when you release the stretch, use Acupressure.

Acupressure Points for a Stitch in the Side.

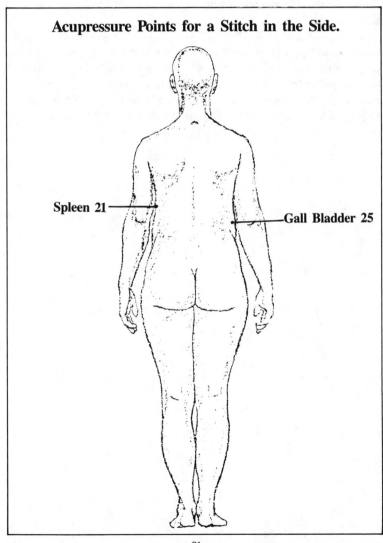

Spleen 21

Gall Bladder 25

Swelling and Carpal Tunnel Syndrome

Many women have swollen hands and feet in late pregnancy. Dr. Tom Brewer, an authority on physiologic edema of late pregnancy says that only a fraction of women who swell will develop toxemia and those who do are often deficient in high-quality protein. If your blood pressure is perfectly normal and there's no protein in your urine (this is determined at your regular prenatal visit), consider yourself healthy. Practice leg exercises, increase protein to 100 grams per day and rest on your left side twice a day for fifteen minutes. It is not yet known whether or not aerobic exercise normalizes blood pressure in pregnancy but fast walking is a safe exercise.

As discussed earlier in Chapter Two, carpal tunnel syndrome causes numbness and pain in the wrists from nerve pressure and, according to some reports, Vitamin B6 deficiency.[1] When you swell in late pregnancy, you may suffer from this problem and in severe cases, surgery may be advised. Try Acupressure and diuretic foods (see Chapter Two) first, if at all possible. Keep your wrists flexible to reduce numbness and pressure.

Exercises for the Wrists

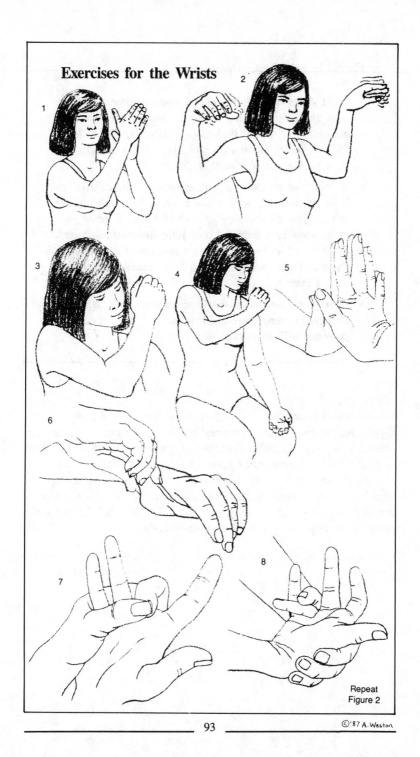

Repeat
Figure 2

93

©'87 A. Weston

Foot Care in Late Pregnancy

- Tight shoes with high heels or wedges promote injury, pain and ankle swelling. High-heeled wedgies are dangerous. Try wearing Birkenstock sandals (Birkenstock, 46 Galli Drive, Novato, CA 94947) or Shakti shoes (Shakti, 6 Export Drive, Sterling, VA 94947).

- Stretch and rotate your ankles to stimulate circulation in the lower legs and feet and prevent fluid buildup. Sit in a chair with your legs stretched out in front of you. Point your toes forward and hold for thirty seconds. Point your toes to your nose for another thirty seconds. Draw a circle with your toes a dozen times in one direction. Reverse.

- Have your partner or a friend massage your legs in a wringing motion from ankle to knee. This type of massage has a fluid release effect.

Shortness of Breath

Shortness of breath during your final trimester can be a problem, even if you have exercised faithfully throughout your pregnancy. Pregnancy increases your oxygen consumption, just as it increases food consumption to meet your developing baby's needs. As your expanding uterus rises, it restricts the movement of the diaphragm. Your lungs are pushed upward slightly, causing an annoying shortness of breath. Swimming and fast walking increases your lung capacity, and you will find it helpful to use the Acupressure points in Chart 19 on a daily basis.

Acupressure Points to Relieve Shortness of Breath

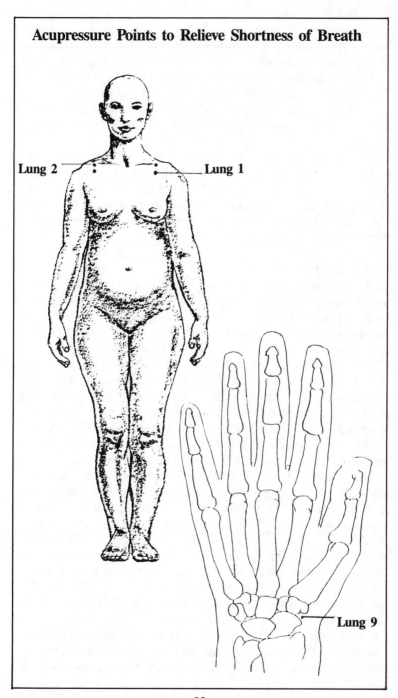

Lung 2

Lung 1

Lung 9

Your Baby's Birth

Pace yourself in the last months to have sufficient energy to attend child-birth education classes and prepare for the work of birthing. Rest and exercise give you the endurance needed for labor. They also counteract pregnancy discomforts and sleep interruptions caused by visits to the bathroom, baby movements and Braxton-Hicks contractions. As you near your due date, use all of your stress reduction skills — including Acupressure — to balance your emotions and remain rested. Fatigue intensifies the pain of labor.

Almost every woman worries about labor pain, especially if she hears horror stories. There is a balance between sticking your head in the sand and absorbing too many disappointing experiences. As you gather information, build up your confidence by acquiring the necessary skills for labor. Cultivate the friendship of women who've had positive births and are well-informed about childbirth politics.

First Stage Labor

First stage labor begins with a show of mucus, or persistent contractions, or rupture of the bag of waters. It ends when your cervix is dilated to ten centimeters. Dr. Lester Hazell, an anthropologist who coached one thousand women in labor, says that your job in the first stage is to relax, breathe slowly and allow your body to do its work.[2]

Ideally, you'll handle half of the first stage in your own home with help from your partner and friends. Natalie walked on the beach, then sat in a warm bath for an hour. Stella listened to music and watched a flickering candle when contractions began to hurt. Both women made sure they were in active labor (dilation to five or six centimeters) before being admitted to the hospital. They'd learned that ambulation throughout labor promotes progress. They also wanted to avoid obstetrical interventions.

Some women refuse the touch therapies when they are in transition (seven to ten centimeters). It takes skill to massage and comfort a woman at this point. Sometimes a hospital nurse or labor coach counsels the partner in what is needed. Natalie felt more secure when her husband's face was nearby. Stella calmed down when the nurse put her hand on her forehead. Do be open with your partner now and show him/her how to touch and comfort you. Be explicit about what you'd like in place of the touch therapies.

The theory of natural childbirth is supported by Selye's fight flight reflex concept. Grantly Dick-Read, a pioneer of natural childbirth, described the reflex as a fear-pain-tension cycle (see Chapter One).[3] Fear or anger floods your body with stress hormones (catecholamines) that weaken your contractions and make labor ineffectual (dystocia). While there are medical reasons for this to happen, it's often a case of psychological dystocia (fear, pain, tension).[4]

Acupressure Points for Birthing

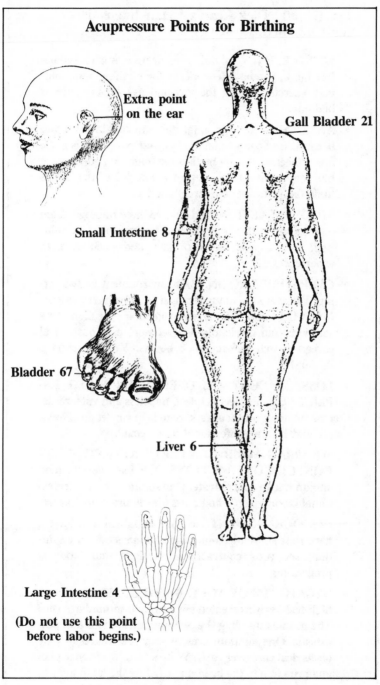

Extra point on the ear

Gall Bladder 21

Small Intestine 8

Bladder 67

Liver 6

Large Intestine 4

(Do not use this point before labor begins.)

Dr. Grantly Dick-Read's "Pain Intensifiers" for Childbirth

- FATIGUE. If you couldn't sleep or were overworked before labor, you have less energy for birthing. One solution: exercise during the day and use Acupressure at bedtime.

- ANEMIA. If your prenatal diet was low in iron, you become tired early in labor and your perineum is more apt to lacerate during birth. One solution: squeeze one-half lemon into a half-cup of prune juice. Drink this tonic daily throughout pregnancy.

- AUTOSUGGESTION. You have received messages from others that birth is painful and frightening. One solution: talk to women who have had positive birth experiences.

- OVERSTIMULATION. Your environment is distracting. There are too many strangers and/or interventions, bright light and noise break your concentration. One solution: find a friendly, low tech-oriented obstetrical caregiver well before labor begins. You can change doctors!

- LOSS OF CONTROL OVER YOUR BIRTH EXPERIENCE. You feel helpless, hopeless and vulnerable. One solution: use Acupressure to help you let go of anxiety and hire a professional labor coach.

- FOCUSING YOUR COMPLETE ATTENTION ON PAINFUL CONTRACTIONS. You feel overwhelmed and unable to concentrate. One solution: hire a professional labor coach who knows how to use Acupressure.

- DISCOURAGEMENT. You are impatient and have a hard time surrendering to the birth process. One solution: see your contractions as signs that labor is progressing.

- NEGATIVITY OF YOUR BIRTH ATTENDANTS. A high-tech, crisis oriented environment intimidates you. The people attending the birthing are anxious and pessimistic. One solution: present your preferences to your obstetrical caregiver early. Write a birth preference plan and present it to the head nurse before the ninth month.

©'87.A.Weston

Second Stage Labor

Whereas the first stage can last a day — fourteen hours is average with a first baby — the second stage or birthing is a matter of one to three hours. You may find the bearing down action of second stage a great relief, although not every woman feels like pushing at ten centimeters (it's all right to take a rest). There will be burning pain at the crowning of the baby's head and you'll need to pant and relax your perineum until your baby is born.

Become acquainted ahead of time with birth equipment. Typically, it consists of a conventional delivery table with stirrups and a back rest. Your partner will be lifting you into a rowboat position with each contraction. Ideally, you'd squat or stand supported by two people. For a hospital birth, negotiate ahead of time to assume the most comfortable position on a conventional delivery table. A side-lying position (right leg in stirrup or sling) takes pressure and pain off your back and allows your partner to rub your back and apply Acupressure. If you do use the customary rowboat position, pull up on the vertical bars with each contraction. Have the stirrups as low and comfortable as possible.

Birthing rooms offer specialized beds that adjust to the upright position like a dental chair. With a Borning bed, you'll be more comfortable using accessory foot rests. The Adele bed allows you to squat directly on the bed holding onto a squatting bar. At home, you can use a beanbag chair to round your back while you're birthing your baby.

The Question About Episiotomy

An episiotomy is an incision made in the muscles between the vagina and anus to speed up a birth. U.S. doctors routinely perform episiotomies. New research does not support the old dictum that episiotomy prevents jagged tears and vaginal relaxation. Some are questioning why we accept a painful wound that makes it hard to care for the baby in the first week and can interfere with sexual relations later.[5]

- To avoid an episiotomy, you need to be in good health and practice Kegels throughout pregnancy and thereafter.

- You must also practice perineal massage during the last six weeks of pregnancy.

- Your efforts must be supported by your physician or midwife. Ideally, she/he will be skilled in perineal massage and the use of hot compresses and oil on the perineum.

- Your efforts must be supported by the hospital staff. You don't want to be hurried.

- You'll need premium coaching to pant for the birth of the baby's head. Your partner must work in tandem with the health professional to remind you what to do.

Third Stage Labor

The third stage begins after the baby is born and ends with the expulsion of the placenta. During this time, you finally meet your baby in person. Skin to skin contact is soothing and promotes bonding. Hold and handle the baby as much as possible during the first hour of life, since a healthy baby often wants to sleep later.

The placenta may slip out while you nurse your baby, or you may have to stand and push it out. Breastfeeding triggers the release of oxytocin which cuts down on bleeding in the third stage. You can help by massaging your uterus until it hardens up under your hand. Keep this up while you're relating to your baby. If there is any problem with excess bleeding or retention of the placenta (this is rare), Acupressure can help you.

An Acupressure Postpartum Recovery Program

After your baby is born, Acupressure self-treatment calms you down, eases any muscular soreness and restores energy. You will need time to recover from the hard work of childbirth. Your uterus will gradually return to its normal size, a process known as involution.

The first ten days, you'll have a red discharge composed of blood and tissue shreddings that lightens in color and amount from day to day. If you breastfeed your baby without any supplements, you may not have a menstrual period for a year. If you partially breastfeed (using bottles and solid foods), you'll probably have a period in three or four months. If you bottlefeed, you'll have a period with or without ovulation in four to eight weeks.

Swollen lymph glands typically cause breast engorgement on the third day after birthing. (See Acupressure Points for Breast Tenderness in Chapter Two.) If you are not planning to nurse, consider applying ice packs to your breasts in place of using medication. Drink sage/alfalfa tea, one teaspoon sage and one teaspoon alfalfa leaf to one cup hot water, to further block the production of breast milk. It can be drunk freely.

Your body may feel stiff and sore. Gentle warm oil massage from a knowledgeable bodyworker feels good at this time. Be sure to make it clear that you have recently given birth and that you need a light touch. Yoga stretches are a safe exercise for you.

Acupressure Points for Postpartum Recovery

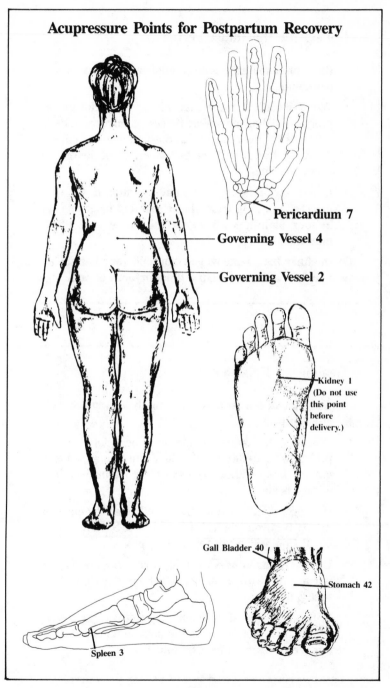

Pericardium 7

Governing Vessel 4

Governing Vessel 2

Kidney 1
(Do not use
this point
before
delivery.)

Gall Bladder 40

Stomach 42

Spleen 3

Caring for the Intact Perineum

- Right after the baby is born, apply an ice pack to your perineum.

- Warm sitzbaths increase circulation to the perineum and promote healing of swolling tissues. Comfrey root baths are a traditional remedy. Put one and one-half cups of dried comfrey root in the bathwater. Sit in the tub for fifteen minutes.

- Ginger root relieves itching and irritation of the vagina. Peel and chop fresh ginger root and place one cup in your bathwater. Sit in the tub for at least fifteen minutes.

With either bath remedy, you can hold your baby while you soak, making a relaxing time for both of you.

Healing an Episiotomy

- Ask your doctor or midwife to apply an icepack right after suturing.

- Change pads frequently and use a heat light on your perineum for twenty minutes three times a day. At home, use any lamp with a sixty-watt bulb. Natural sunlight is very healing.

- Do Kegel exercises immediately following the episiotomy. At first you will feel stiff and sore. Soon increased blood flow will begin the healing process.

- Use warm sitzbaths twice a day. Itchy, dry wounds feel much better with an application of wheat germ or Vitamin E oil.

- With large, painful episiotomies, get off your feet every two or three hours. Nurse the baby on your side. Rotate ice packs with heat treatments.

The postpartum period is a time of emotional challenge. You may feel tired and overwhelmed after the excitement of birthing. Involution can be a major letdown after the "high" of having a baby. Ask your partner and friends to help you minimize other responsibilities while you recover your energy and strengthen your connection with your baby.

Breastfeeding

Successful breastfeeding is dependent upon your ability to release a steady flow of milk that supports your child's growth and development. It's now acknowledged that human milk is more digestible, has a higher iron uptake, reduces the risk of allergy and meets unique emotional needs of mother and child. Women find Acupressure self-care lends itself easily to nursing. Acupressure reduces any tension in the muscles that support your breasts and its relaxing effect encourages a reflex mechanism essential for giving your baby milk.

The milk ejection reflex or "letdown" that releases milk when the baby suckles. Suckling triggers the pituitary gland to secrete oxytocin, which also contracts your uterus in labor. In turn, oxytocin stimulates your breasts to let down milk. Letdown or milk ejection reflex is sabotaged by stress in any form.

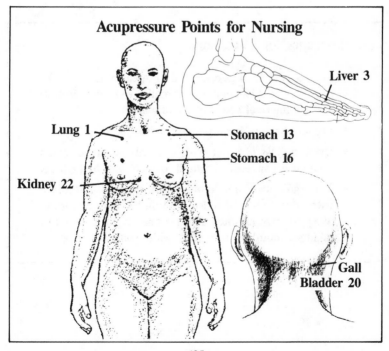

Acupressure Points for Nursing

Liver 3

Lung 1

Stomach 13

Stomach 16

Kidney 22

Gall Bladder 20

Nature, it seems, intended the human infant to receive milk from his/her mother. The eminent anthropologist, Dr. Ashley Montagu, suggests that the newborn is an "immature product," born before the rapidly-growing brain becomes too large to pass through a woman's body. After birth, this baby is still programmed to have his/her needs met with a minimum of effort. Montagu considers the age of nine months to be the time when this child is capable of making a greater effort in his/her own behalf.[6] Indeed, this is when many children begin to walk. Karen Pryor, a scientist who studied human lactation, says this is when spontaneous weanings occur.[7]

While this hypothesis is attractive, you as a modern mother (often living in isolation from helpful relatives) cannot breastfeed your baby without being well cared for yourself. Fatigue, worry and poor nutrition will undermine your nursing efforts. Like pregnancy, nursing makes demands upon your body. You are still eating for two — and then some. Do take a vitamin supplement designed for lactating mothers and two grams of calcium a day. You'll have more vitality by increasing your intake of the B-complex, either with supplements or in natural foods such as whole-grain products. You require six to eight glasses of liquid per day. It won't be hard to consume this much. Nursing is thirst-making work. Make a habit of having something to drink every time you nurse your baby.

Beverages for Lactation

- Keep a pitcher of peppermint or spearmint tea in the refrigerator. Avoid caffeine (it makes your baby fretful) and commercial sodas of all kinds.

- Prepare or buy freshly-made carrot juice.

- Drink a glass of water with a freshly squeezed lemon (don't use a sweetener). You'll soon get used to the taste.

- The traditional tonic to build milk supply is dill mixed with equal parts of anise seed and sweet marjoram. Steep for five minutes and use one or two cups daily, taking a mouthful at a time while you're nursing.

Engorgement and Sore Nipples

In a natural setting, women nursed their babies without looking at the clock. There was no concern about feeding times and engorgement was a rarity. Today hospital personnel frequently warn you to keep the baby at breast for a specified amount of time or you'll suffer from sore nipples later. To avoid engorgement and rock-hard breasts on the third day, learn how to hand express. Use this skill to soften the areola so that the baby can grasp both the nipple and the areola. Chewing on the nipple, which the baby is apt to do if the area is swollen, causes pain. If you do become engorged, call a La Leche League leader or a breastfeeding counselor for help. In the meantime, apply heat in a tub or shower to give relief and bring "let-down" of your milk. Both nipple pain and engorgement are time-limited problems that require immediate attention. The crisis will soon pass, and nursing will become a pleasure.

Exhaustion

"Losing sleep," Natalie says, "is a fringe benefit of parenthood." Between feedings, Stella wonders whether she'll ever have a full night of rest. If you are like these mothers, you'll be semi-exhausted during the early weeks of motherhood. Your body is healing from childbirth. You are learning how to breastfeed and care for a baby. Your time is no longer your own. Putting the baby on a bottle is usually not the answer. This can be more time-consuming than nursing. Still, you need your rest.

Learn to prioritize your time in order to get enough sleep. Minimize household tasks, bring the baby to bed with you and rally a support network. In earlier days, some cultures assigned a "doula" or wise woman to care for the new mother during the postpartum period to build up her strength. Today there are doula services in some communities. Consider this service a part of your Acupressure self-care. Press points to calm your emotions and make this a relaxed, reflective time.

Reference Notes
1. Carpal Tunnel Syndrome, an Inexpensive Alternative to a $3,000 Operation, *Healthfacts*, September 1986.
2. Hazell, Lester, *COMMONSENSE CHILDBIRTH*, out of print.
3. Grantly Dick-Read, *CHILDBIRTH WITHOUT FEAR*, fourth edition, revised by Helen Wessel and Harlan F. Ellis, M.D., Harper and Row, 1972.
4. Baldwin, Rahima, *PREGNANT FEELINGS*, Celestial Arts, 1986.
5. Cohen, Nancy, *SILENT KNIFE*, Bergin and Garvey, 1983.
6. Montague, Ashley, "Neonatal and Infant Immaturity in Man," *Journal of the American Medical Association*, October 1961.
7. Pryor, Karen, *NURSING YOUR BABY*, Harper and Row, 1973.

CHAPTER FIVE
Menopause and Aging

Menopause means — literally — the cessation of menstruation which occurs on the average at age fifty-one, but ranges from the early forties to the mid-fifties. The process of menopause is not complete until you've missed twelve consecutive periods. As your ovaries slow down their estrogen production, your periods may stop abruptly, gradually or irregularly, with or without troublesome symptoms over a period of one to ten years. During this time, a light menstruation, a missed period, or unusually heavy periods may be part of a natural process. According to Dr. Niles Newton of Northwestern University, it can be quite normal for you to flood on the first menstrual day (of course, you want to screen out any bleeding-related problems with regular gynecological check-ups and Pap smears).[1]

Biological Influences

As you get older, your ovaries gradually decrease in size and function (ovarian regression). Before menopause, they produce monthly waves of estrogen (see Chapter Two) that maintain tone in your breasts and vagina (among other functions). Thus, your estrogen supply remains relatively constant until the onset of menopause, except during pregnancy (when it rises) and lactation (when it falls). Even in menopause, your diminishing supply of estrogen is supplemented by androstanedione, a substance produced by the adrenal glands. Your ovaries continue to secrete androgens (male hormones) which help maintain your sex drive, muscular strength and cardiovascular endurance. (Women produce small amounts of androgens. Men produce small amounts of estrogen.)

Ovarian regression is a contributing cause of hot flashes, vaginal and bladder changes, and bone thinning that puts some older women at higher risk for osteoporosis. (Estrogen is a key ingredient in building bone mass.) Keep in mind, however, that until the recent push to treat menopausal symptoms as dis-ease, only twenty percent of all mid-life women sought medical help for troublesome symptoms. Sixty percent reported only minor problems which they could handle themselves, and another twenty percent experienced no problems whatsoever.[2]

Psychological Influences

Medical science defines menopause as a deficiency dis-ease and prescribes estrogen replacement hormones. This illness-oriented perspective is reinforced by drug advertisements in gynecology journals that portray older women as anxious individuals who are a burden to themselves and others.[3] Yet, like many others, you may feel intense relief when monthly periods end. You no longer need to worry about birth control or the possibility of unwanted pregnancy. Sex can be better than ever. Although menopause is supposed to make you irrational and overemotional, large numbers of women described themselves as productive, self-confident and satisfied with life. Depression, irritability and other signs of low self-esteem (including the much-discussed empty nest syndrome) can occur at any stage in life.

The menopausal years are an opportunity to put all of the energy and skill you developed by caring for others to work for yourself. Menopause occurs at the peak of your vigor and experience in dealing with the world and coincides with the age that your children attain maturity. A flood of menopausal women are entering the job market and making new lives for themselves.

The famous mystery writer, Agatha Christie, once commented that a woman did not really become herself until age fifty. Many modern women agree. When Rebecca re-entered the job market, she was astonished to win out over younger competitors because, she was told, her mature judgment would be a valuable asset to the company. Helen, a pediatric nurse, earned a certificate in Swedish massage the day before she turned fifty. Her new skill added an interesting dimension to the job she'd held for a quarter of a century. In the hospital, she became known for her special ability to calm sleepless, frightened children.

Social Influences

Jane Porcino refers to menopause as "uncharted territory."[4] At the turn of the century, female life expectancy was forty-eight and only a fraction of women lived beyond "the change" that ended the childbearing years. Typically, a woman was a wife and mother for half a century without having to adjust to new and different roles. In contrast, you'll have many role choices to make in living out the thirty years that follow menopause. Much of your satisfaction depends upon your financial security, spiritual outlook and health.

Chinese women and men traditionally began the daily practice of Tai Chi Chu'an in their late fifties to maintain joint flexibilty and increase energy. You can also better your health in the later years by following an Acupressure-based self-care program that includes regular exercise.

Reducing Stress During the Menopause

Stress worsens your menopausal experience. Financial difficulties and divorce shock are major causes of depression in the middle years. To problem-solve through a midlife crisis:

• Become clear emotionally and get direction from a capable woman therapist or support group for menopausal women, if you're having trouble with relationships.

• Begin to take care of yourself financially. Learn about wills, trusts and investments, so that you can make intelligent decisions.

• Upgrade your marketable skills if necessary. Job training is available at most community colleges. Universities are usually very encouraging to older women seeking degrees.

• Seek a career counselor before embarking upon any education program. Check with the Young Women's Christian Association (YWCA), the American Association of University Women (AAUW) or the National Organization of Women (NOW) for referrals. Meet the counselor with two lists, one titled "My Accomplishments" and the other, "My Possibilities." Be sure to include all of your talents and achievements (the mural you painted on your daughter's wall, the tire you changed last week, and any volunteer work).

Hot Flashes

The hot flash is the best known and most dreaded sign of menopause. As hormones rearrange themselves in midlife, you may experience this painless rush of heat that suffuses your upper body for a few seconds to two minutes. Hot flashes or flushes may occur four to six times a day — or four to six times an hour and appear with the greatest frequency in the evening when body temperature is at its peak. Sometimes hot flashes and sweating wake you up at night.

Hot flashes occur in forty to seventy-five percent of all menopausal women. Two explanation are offered, both speculative due to lack of research. First, menopause changes nerve cell tissues (autonomic ganglia) in the hypothalmus, a gland in the brain that also regulated body temperature. A second explanation cites extra amounts of LSH and FSH (see Chapter Three) secreted in an unsuccessful attempt to make the ovaries produce estrogen at levels equal to the childbearing years.[5] No one knows why some menopausal women never have a hot flash. (Symptoms don't always correlate with hormone levels.) The reflex is more troublesome with an abrupt menopause, especially when the ovaries are surgically removed (this effect is absent in younger women, for unknown reasons). There is also a rebound effect after discontinuing estrogen replacement hormones, noted in one woman who had hot flashes lasting 2.4 to 4.6 minutes. These unusually long flashes were uncomfortable but body temperature never rose about dangerous levels.[6]

Healthy, happy women do have hot flashes, but it's more of a problem for chronically stressed, under-exercised and/or poorly nourished women. Hot flashes are more severe in smokers (smoking affects the circulation) and in women with vitamin E deficiency.

Herbal Treatment of Hot Flashes

- Motherwort is traditionally used to regulate the temperature during the menopausal years. Prepare Motherwort by steeping one teaspoon of the leaves in one-half cup boiling water for ten minutes. Drink a mouthful at a time and do not exceed one-half cup per day.

- Dong quai is an age-old Chinese tonic for women. Steep one teaspoon of this sleep-inducing herb in one cup of hot water for ten minutes. Drink one or two cups before bedtime.

Rosetta Reitz (see Recommended Readings), a pioneer in demystifying the menopause, interviewed 500 women about their hot flashes. None had missed work, even with heavy sweating; nor did hot flashes last over two minutes. Ten percent complained of a slight chill following a hot flash, and nearly all said flushing was more bothersome when they were stressed.[7]

Reitz and Dr. Sadja Greenwood recommended a holistic approach stressing self-help and a commonsense attitude toward the actual hot flash. Dr. Greenwood added many practical suggestions. The caffeine in coffee or black tea raises your metabolism (see Chapter Three). Alcohol also makes you warm and increases flushing. Hot baths, saunas and heavy blankets can aggravate the hot flash reflex. If you share a bed, purchase an electric blanket with two sets of controls. When overheated, run cool water over your feet and have something to drink. (A thermos or bota bag is easily carried.)

Acupressure Points for Relief of Hot Flashes

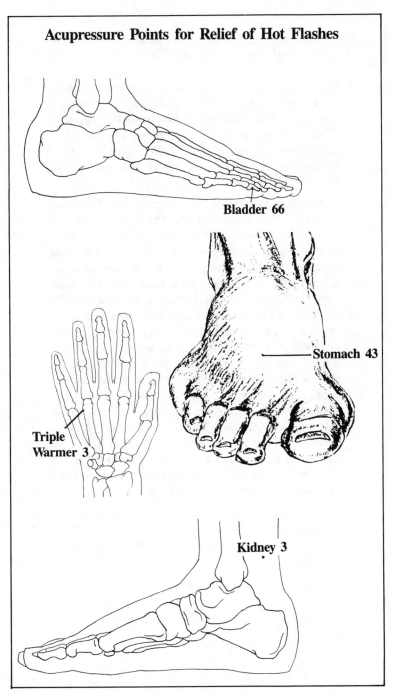

Bladder 66

Stomach 43

Triple Warmer 3

Kidney 3

Pros and Cons of Using Estrogen Replacement Hormones (ERH)

- **PROS:** ERH is the treatment of choice for menopausal women. Doctors say ERH is safer than previously, as over-stimulating estrogens are balanced with progestins. ERH is effective in relieving symptoms associated with hot flashes and vaginal and bladder problems. It also reduces the risk of osteoporosis, a bone dis-ease responsible for the high fracture rate in older women.

- **CONS:** Hormones are frequently prescribed for healthy womenm, despite reported side-effects. The use of ERH changes over forty metabolic functions. ERH can be habit-forming and requires constant medical management and expensive tests. Women find it hard to terminate ERH, as symptoms sometimes recur when treatment is discontinued. ERH causes a return of monthly bleeding and is a known danger to women with breast or vaginal cancers, abnormal vaginal bleeding, thrombophlebitis or embolism, varicose veins, liver dis-ease, fibroid tumors, hypertension, smoking addiction or obesity. Estrogen given alone for menopause increased the risk of endometrial cancer six to eight times. Other studes associate ERH with a higher risk of breast cancer.

    If you decide to take ERH, ask your doctor about the transdermal patch, approved by the FDA in 1986. With the patch, the hormones seep into your body through the skin, instead of being processed by the liver where they alter so many body functions.

Vaginal and Bladder Changes

Vaginal changes caused by thinning of the vaginal walls (occurring in half of all menopausal women) include vaginal dryness, itching and, in about twenty percent, intercourse pain. (Estrogen cream is used to puff up the vaginal tissues and make intercourse more comfortable. However, estrogen cream is absorbed into the bloodstream and has the same risks as estrogens given by mouth.) You may notice frequent urination and an increased number of vaginal and bladder infections. Urinary incontinence can cause you to lose urine when you laugh or sneeze.

Tests that determine the degree of vaginal thinning include the maturation index (an analysis of vaginal cells) and the plasma estrogen. Neither consistently correlates to the other or matches your symptoms (or lack thereof). Therefore, you may want to try a few home remedies — and Acupressure (see Chapter Three) — for troublesome symptoms, before you submit to expensive tests of this kind.

Begin now to maintain vaginal health and reduce the likelihood of infection by keeping your sugar intake low and practicing the Kegel exercise faithfully. Avoid douches and bath products which contain chemical irritants. At bedtime, apply wheat germ or coconut oil to the inside of your vagina. (Do not use petroleum-based products, like vaseline). Follow good bathroom hygiene, and use Acupressure points to promote vaginal lubrication and bladder health. Orgasm is strongly recommended to tone the vagina and surrounding tissues.

Your sexuality can blossom in mid-life if you use a sensual (i.e., slower) approach. Enhance your sexual development with massage, the use of erotic and a wider exploration of sexual practices. However, there is less estrogen to produce sexual fluids, and you may have difficulty with intercourse. Unless you understand and solve the problem, your relationship may be weakened and your sexual confidence undermined.

These adaptations will help the lubrication. Incorporate the use of lubricants (any vegetable oil) when you begin to make love. Allow at least five minutes for penetration, while the penis is gradually inserted, preferably in conjunction with clitoral stimulation.

Vaginal health is promoted by orgasm, which may be achieved by techniques other than coitus.

Kegel Exercise

Squeeze muscles around your anus, vagina and bladder opening tightly, as if you were stopping a flow of urine, then release. Repeat. The Kegel vaginal squeeze should be done at least 100 times per day. Each squeeze takes less than one second. Do the squeeze anywhere: in bed, at a stoplight, standing in line. Do not Kegel on a full bladder.

Practiced diligently, the Kegel exercise can strengthn the muscles around your bladder to give you more control.

Marshmallow root (also known as althea) is a classic remedy for urinary incontinence. Steep one cup of the dried root to one cup of boiling hot water and drink one to two cupfuls per day.

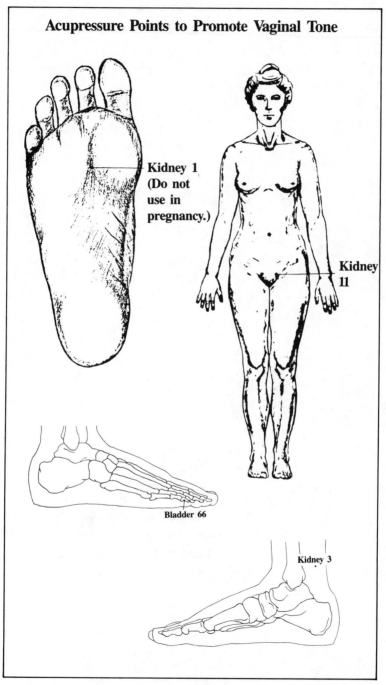

Acupressure Points to Promote Vaginal Tone

Kidney 1
(Do not
use in
pregnancy.)

Kidney
11

Bladder 66

Kidney 3

Acupressure Points for Bladder Health

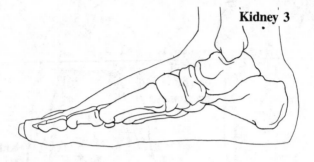

Kidney 3

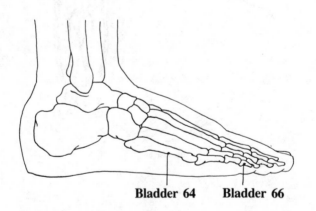

Bladder 64   Bladder 66

Osteoporosis Prevention

Aging involves a certain amount of bone thinning. However, osteoporosis can weaken your bones to the extent that they easily fracture. (It is common to hear about an aging woman falling and fracturing a hip; what is less known is that the fracture could have occurred before she fell.) If you have osteoporosis, you may develop a curve at the top of your spine called "dowager's hump" and lose inches of height. There can also be back pain from compressed vertebrae. In some women, osteoporosis can also loosen teeth.

Health-conscious women should concern themselves with osteoporosis prevention early in life. After age thirty, when your bones start losing mass, increase your intake of calcium and keep up a weight bearing exercise program. Your bones are constantly forming and breaking down under the influence of mineral and hormone interactions. As part of this process, your body is always storing and withdrawing calcium from the bones. Since calcium is also a vital ingredient for other body functions (like blood clotting), your bones may have to yield their supply if you're calcium-deficient. There is also a calcium drain during pregnancy and breastfeeding, as well as after menopause.

Doctors often prescribe ERH in early menopause to prevent osteoporosis (see "Pros and Cons of ERH"). However, calcium supplementation, exercise and Acupressure to tonify bone structure can be a safer approach in low-risk women.

One-fourth of all women over sixty have osteoporosis. It is more likely to occur in small-boned, white postmenopausal women who are underexercised and/or deficient in vitamin D and calcium. The overall fracture rate in elderly women is still only one in five. Starting an osteoporosis prevention program in your thirties will help you to remain vigorous and active throughout your life.

Calcium and Bone Health

• It's hard to get a daily gram or more of calcium without adding unwanted calories. Low-calorie, calcium-rich foods include low-fat yogurt, canned salmon and sardines, sesame seeds, dark green leafy vegetables and tofu (see Chapter Two). If you have kidney problems, consult your doctor before you take calcium supplements.

• Calcium absorption slows with age. Calcium salts (calcium lactate or gluconate) are absorbed most efficiently when taken with milk and Vitamin D. Do not exceed 400 units of Vitamin D per day. Exposure to sun also increases your body's supply of Vitamin D.

• Alcohol, nicotine, coffee and salt interfere with calcium absorption. It is currently speculated that phosphorus (large amounts of phosphorus are found in red meats and soft drinks) has a similar effect.

Acupressure Points for Bone Health

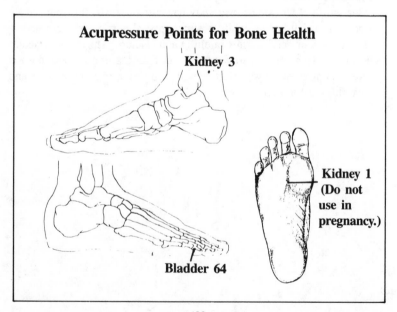

Kidney 3

Kidney 1
(Do not use in pregnancy.)

Bladder 64

The Aging Woman

The first rule of health for the aging woman is to disregard the stereotype. Pamela Valois, who photographed vigorous, interesting women aged seventy and older, describes an essay by Elizabeth Janeway, "Breaking the Age Barrier," that criticizes a picture of the older woman as sick and poor, instead of healthy and fulfilled. Her collaborator, Charlotte Painter (see Recommended Reading), wrote biographies of these inspiring women. She stated that they were often more passionate about work than ever before and maintained enormous interest in life.[8]

Begin now — whatever your age — to question the stereotype. If you're fifty (or older) challenge the prejudice against against aging women by thinking of yourself as an interesting and worthwhile "elder." Never apologize for your age — even in jest. Cultivate a circle of friends who share your realistic yet optimistic approach to aging. Many educated, older women remain independent and active. Jane Porcino, author of *Growing Older, Getting Better,* states that women today are enjoying sports and learning new skills in the seventh and eighth decades of life (see Recommended Reading).

If you feel victimized by your age, you will find that direct, constructive action is the best therapy. Get involved with special interest groups that work in your behalf. Find a way to continue meaningful work. Margarethe, an ex-language teacher, built a part-time career by providing interpreting services for physicians and dentists. Laura, who raised three happy and independent adults, took in a foster child. A young restaurant owner gratefully acknowledged help received from members of the Service Corps of Retired Executives (SCORE).

Aging and Health

The way that you use your time and your mind undeniably affects your health. For example, it's now proven that memory loss is more likely to be caused by lack of physical and mental exercise than by hardening of the arteries.[9] Much of what you consider "senility" is caused by isolation and the effects of painkillers and sedatives that interfere with short-term memory. If you're retired, it's essential to "exercise" your mind, by pursuing volunteer work, an avocation and/or returning to college. Health is promoted by meaningful activity and the sense that what you do makes a difference in the world.

You're also more apt to be in the high-level wellness category if your diet supplies required nutrients. Older people are frequently deficient in Vitamins A, B complex, and C, and in the minerals: calcium, iron, and magnesium. These deficiencies lower immunity and cause many age-associated problems — frequent infections, headaches, irritability, depression and sleep problems. People over age sixty often lack Vitamin A, which maintains the health of the skin, eyes, and mucus membrane and strengthens resistance to dis-ease. (Many prescribed drugs, notably estrogens, diuretics and anti-inflammatory medications, interfere with absorption of vitamins and minerals.)

If you're like most women, you want to age gracefully. Most older women fear death less than disability and helplessness. A program of self-treatment — and Acupressure — boosts your ability to live independently within any physical limitations. If you have a health problem, you can make more intelligent healthcare decisions, combining self-care with appropriate medical treatment.

It's never too late to begin to change your health habits. Acupressure is particularly helpful during the second half of your life, and learning to press points is an excellent way to exercise body and mind. Begin now to press points (see Introduction, "How to Press Points") for any of the following: heart problems, muscular-skeletal stiffness and pain, bone diseases and stress symptoms.

A Healthy Heart

In Asian medical philosophy, the heart is often referred to as the Supreme Controller or Administrator, because its function is vital to survival. In this school, the heart is the center of love for yourself and others. When you "take heart," you are strong, full of energy, alive with interest in life. When you "lose heart," you feel discouraged and negative about yourself. Having heart is a step in lowering your risk for heart dis-ease. You as a postmenopausal woman are considered at higher risk, especially when you're under-exercised or "broken-hearted." The drop in your estrogen supply changes the way your body uses cholesterol. The "good" lipo-proteins (high density) that function to break down dietary cholesterol are lowered. The "bad" lipo-proteins (low-density) that channel cholesterol into blood vessels where they can form plaque are increased. However, there are many dietary changes you can make to counteract this action. For example, brewer's yeast, a concentrated food, lowers cholesterol when taken daily.

Hypertension is a "silent killer" that's associated with stress and a sedentary life. Some elevation of blood pressure in older people is normal but a consistently high reading is suspicious. (You can monitor your blood pressure at home, but consult a health professional if you experience any eye changes, dizziness or numbness in your limbs. Equipment to monitor your blood pressure can be ordered from Medical Self-Care, Box 1000, Inverness, CA 94956.) If you're sedentary and stress-ridden, you're at greater risk for hypertension. Cardiovascular exercise (activity which makes your heart pound and induces sweating) may prevent and reduce high blood pressure. A health professional can show you how to monitor pulse rate checks according to your age and weight.

A program of holistic self-care which emphasizes stress reduction can be used to prevent hypertension. Acupressure is the cornerstone of the program. In 1984, the National Institute of Health issued the recommendation that relaxation therapy should be the first treatment for mild hypertension. Relaxation training had an effect similar to results seen with drugs called "beta blockers," specific for lowering blood pressure.[10]

The Acupressure points in Chart 31 energize your heart and circulatory functions. For maximum benefit, use these points before heart trouble becomes a concern. However, even with heart dis-ease, you can begin using Acupressure along with medical treatment.

Acupressure Points to Tonify the Heart

If you are using more than one point on the Heart meridian, proceed in the order given below:

1. Heart 1
2. Heart 7
3. Pericardium 7
4. Conception Vessel 17

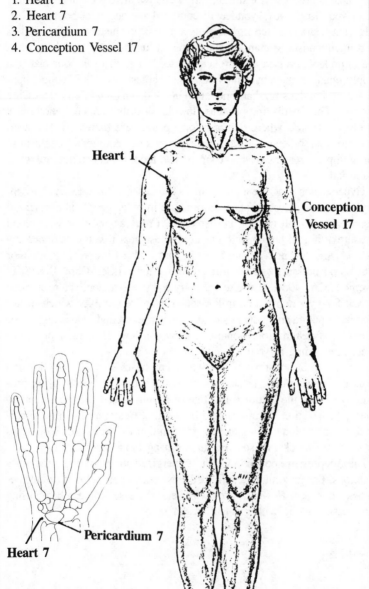

Heart 1

Conception Vessel 17

Pericardium 7

Heart 7

Taking Heart

No matter how healthy your lifestyle, grief or loss can slow you down and cause you to lose heart. Grief normally follows loss: through the death of a beloved partner or friend.

- Healing yourself requires a period of mourning to work through various stages of anger and depression. Do allow yourself the time to grieve. Chronic, unacknowledged grief can threaten your health.

- Reconstructing life after loss is easier when you have a strong social network. Friends are a potent medicine.

- Prayer and meditation help to restore emotional and spiritual health, one step at a time.

- Transform your grief experience into creativity. Bereaved Hispanic women stitched elaborate samplers in memory of deceased relatives. The sampler's completion marked the end of mourning.

Do "take heart" in order to renew your zest for life and maintain health. As a post-menopausal woman, you suffer an increased risk of heart dis-ease; in some experts' opinions, being "broken hearted" is a precursor to serious illness.

However, you have many opportunities to counteract a tendency to heart dis-ease. If you smoke, you can quit. Aerobic exercise strengthens your cardiovascular system and lowers serum cholesterol. Nutrients like Brewer's yeast, Vitamin E, Vitamin C, and fish liver oils (in sardines and old-fashioned cod liver oil) lower the "bad" lipo-proteins and increase the "good."

The American Heart Association advises you to lose weight if necessary and stop smoking to keep a healthy heart. According to the AHA, fat should account for only thirty percent of your total caloric intake, and salt should be limited to one teaspoon per day. The AHA also recommends that over half (fifty-five percent) of your diet consist of whole grains, fruits and vegetables.

Muscular-Skeletal Stiffness

Muscular-skeletal problems may lead to disabilities that can sharply reduce the quality of your life. Joint pain and stiffness are sometimes severe enough to "bench" you, limiting your movement and causing isolation. Arthritis is a major cause of muscular skeletal stiffness in older people. While there are at least one hundred types of arthritis, the most frequently reported is osteoarthritis, a dis-ease caused by wearing away of the cartilage which protects your joints. Obesity aggravates osteoarthritis by putting an extra burden on the joints, particularly the hips and knees. Acupressure self-help is not a cure, but it can augment medical treatment by promoting muscular relaxation and circulation.

Stiffness and injuries are also caused by poor body mechanics. You can improve posture, although it may mean breaking lifetime habits. Sitting for long periods of time stresses your backbone. If you sit at a desk, make a point of getting up and walking at least once every hour. Sleeping on your stomach weakens your back, and makes you more prone to aching muscles. Twisting or reaching beyond your limits for objects can cause injury. Ask a friend or relative to help you place frequently-used articles, such as cooking utensils, within easy reach.

If you've been treated for arthritis or other muscular-skeletal problems and still have pain and stiffness, you can try yoga stretches and other safe home remedies to ease muscle spasm and pain.

Home Remedies for Joint Pain and Stiffness

Home remedies are not a substitute for medical treatment. If you're injured or suffering, see a health professional before experimenting with self-treatment.

- Apply alternating hot and cold compresses. Place a hot washrag (don't burn yourself!) on the afflicted joint or muscle for five minutes. Replace with an ice pack, keeping it in place another five minutes. Repeat if necessary.

- Start your day with walking or swimming to work out stiffness and stimulate circulation.

- Sit in chairs that allow your feet to be flat on the floor and your knees slightly higher than your hips. If necessary, put a stool or telephone books under your feet.

- Use a pillow in the curve of your back when you drive. When you get out of the car, swing your body around to face the street. Plant both feet on the street. (Do not get in and out of the car swiveling on one leg!) Plant one foot on the road. Put one foot forward, lean over your thigh and rise, bracing yourself with the other foot.

Skin Changes and Appearance

You do not need an expensive collection of cosmetics, despite advertising claims. The cosmetic industry survives by shaming women for bearing the natural effects of time and gravity on the complexion. It is normal for wrinkles to begin when the deepest skin layer (epidermis) loses elasticity and top layers loosen. This process is aggravated by the slowdown of oil-producing glands.

Anything that improves circulation will help your skin and regular exercise is your best toner. Also gently use a stiff natural sponge or loofah to stimulate circulation and plain water to cleanse your face. Apply your favorite moisturizers (preferably with a vegetable oil base) and at night, coat your face with nourishing wheat germ oil (unless you're allergic to wheat) or olive oil and aloe vera cream.

Protect your skin with PABA, Vitamin E oil or another natural sunscreen when you're out in the sun.

Facial tension can aggravate the growth of lines and wrinkles, as it blocks the flow of blood to the skin. Use the Acupressure points in Chart 33 to ease tension and promote circulation in your face, shoulders and neck.

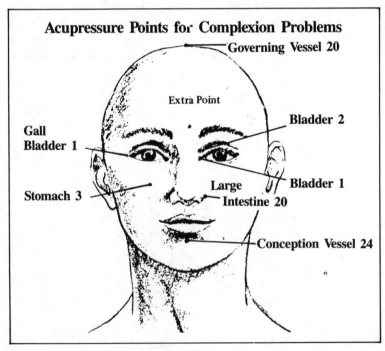

Acupressure Points for Complexion Problems

Governing Vessel 20

Extra Point

Bladder 2

Gall
Bladder 1

Stomach 3

Large
Intestine 20

Bladder 1

Conception Vessel 24

Natural Bath Products

The hormonal changes of menopause make your skin more sensitive. Your regular shampoos, soap or cosmetic products may suddenly cause a rash or itching. Try substituting products which come directly from nature.

- Papaya leaves are an old West Indian substitute for soap. Scrub your skin with the leaves. (A health food store can order these for you.)

- Soap bulb grows freely in the foothills of California's Sierra Nevada. With a mortar and pestle, mash the fresh root and mix with warm water to form a lather for soap or shampoo.

- Yucca plant is another natural shampoo which makes your hair shine. Soak a cup of the chopped roots in four cups of hot water. Let stand overnight, strain and store.

- Lovage root (also known as borage) adds a pleasing scent to your bathwater. Add about one-quarter cup of the dried root to your bathwater. Also try dried orris root, rosemary leaves and lavender flowers.

- Toss a half-teaspoon of sesame or safflower oil into your bath to soften dry skin.

Poor Circulation

Sluggish circulation is one cause of many symptoms of aging: cold hands and feet, general aches and pains and stiff joints. Painful varicose veins are also aggravated by poor circulation. A strong, steady flow of blood throughout your entire body is an essential component of your well-being. When your circulation is active, you feel strong and alert. Wounds heal quickly and you rarely get bruises.

Muscular tension contributes to circulatory problems. If your shoulders are chronically knotted with tension, the flow of blood is impeded and hands become cold and sometimes pale in color. Your lower body, particularly your feet, are even more apt to have poor circulation due to gravity. Many women store tension in their hips. This blocks circulation of blood in the lower body. Acupressure points are very helpful in reducing muscular tension. If you feel your circulatory problems are due to tension in your muscles and joints, you will probably benefit from a daily program of stretching and Acupressure self-care.

Lack of exercise is the number one cause of poor circulation. It is all too easy to fall into a sedentary lifestyle as you age. Vigorous activity speeds up your heart rate, pumping an increased supply of blood. This can do much to improve your overall well being.

Helen complained of cold hands and feet, especially at night. Her acupressurist suggested a daily walk. This was enough to "get her moving" and she reported that she "had more energy" and "just felt like doing more" on the days that she took the time to walk for an hour. Soon, Helen was able to sleep without wearing socks or piling on blankets.

Constipation may also aggravate poor circulation in the hips, legs and feet. The weight of accumulated fecal matter often increases the pain of varicose veins.

Natural Remedies for Constipation

Constipation at any age is a tiresome and embarassing problem. Costly drugstore remedies may have unforeseen side effects.

Constipation is caused by a lack of bulk in your diet, emotional upset and lack of exercise. Iron and calcium supplements may also be temporarily constipating.

- Ripe grapes are a natural laxative.

- Jalap is a Mexican plant which can be obtained at a health store or herb specialty shop. Its roots are used as a bowel cleanser. Steep one teaspoon of the dried root in one cup of hot water. Let it stand till the water is cool. Drink the cup a mouthful at a time, throughout the day. Do not drink more than one cup per day or three cups per week. Jalap is a strong laxative which should not be used if you are pregnant.

- Carrot juice has a laxative effect. It can be made in a home juicer or purchased fresh at a health food store.

Acupressure Points for Constipation

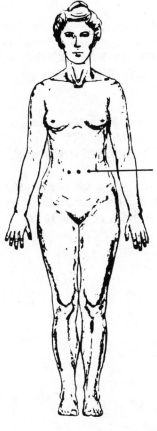

Stomach 25

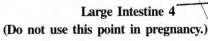

Large Intestine 4
(Do not use this point in pregnancy.)

Reference Notes

1. Newton, Niles, "Overview of the Social, Psychological, and Research Issues in the Psychology of Hysterectomy," *Address at the Proceedings of the Fifth International Congress of Psychosomatic Obstetrics and Gynecology*, Rome, 1977.
2. Seaman, Barbara, et al., *WOMEN AND THE CRISIS IN SEX HORMONES*, Rawson Associates, 1977.
3. Moyer, Linda, "What Obstetrical Journal Advertising Tells About Doctors and Women," *Birth and the Family Journal*, Winter 1976-6.
4. Porcino, Jane, *GETTING OLDER, GROWING BETTER, A HANDBOOK FOR WOMEN IN THE SECOND HALF OF LIFE*, Addison-Wesley, 1983.
5. Seaman, *op. cit.*
6. Molnar, George, "Body Temperatures During Menopausal Hot Flashes," *Journal of Applied Physiology*, March 1975.
7. Reitz, Rosetta, *MENOPAUSE: A POSITIVE APPROACH*, Chilton Book Company, 1977.
8. Painter, Charlotte, *GIFTS OF AGE*, Chronicle Books, 1985.
9. Frankfurter Allgemeine, "Old Age and Arteries Seldom to Blame for Bad Memory," *Health Fitness Nutrition Fact News*, July 1986.
10. Goleman, Daniel, "Relaxation Training Helps the Body Heal," *San Francisco Chronicle*, August 6, 1986.

APPENDICES

APPENDIX I

GLOSSARY

Acupressure A bodywork system in which fingertip pressure is applied to Acupuncture points and meridians.

Acupressure point A specific place on a meridian. Pressure is applied at Acupressure points to affect the state of the energy in the meridians.

Acupuncture A healing system in which silver and gold needles are inserted at specific points on the body.

Adrenal glands A pair of glands located above the kidney, which secrete hormones.

Adrenalin A hormone which stimulates the heart, providing a rush of energy.

Affirmations Positive statements which influence your thoughts and actions in order to achieve desired results.

Anatomical inch The distance between the first and second knuckles. This is the measurement which is used to determine Acupuncture and Acupuncture point locations.

Androgens Hormones which maintain your cardiovascular endurance, muscular strength, sex drive and vaginal flexibility and lubrication.

Androstanedione A substance, produced by your adrenal glands, which your body converts into estrogen as needed.

Anemia A dis-ease in which the blood is deficient in iron, red blood cells or total volume.

Anovulatory bleeding Vaginal bleeding in the absence of ovulation.

Antibody Substances produced by the body which neutralize toxins, enabling it to resist dis-ease.

Areola The colored area surrounding the nipples.

Auditory Relating to hearing.

Bodywork Therapeutic effort which involves movement or manipulation of your body.

Carpal Tunnel Syndrome A condition which involves swelling, numbness and sometimes pain in the wrists.

Catecholamines Stress hormones that are secreted during your "fight or flight" response.

Cervical The vertebrae of the neck or relating to the cervix.

Cervix The opening of the uterus.

Cholesterol A fat-like compound capable of forming plaques that clog your arteries.

Chronic Present or nearly always present.

Cyst A sac which develops abnormally on a cavity or structure of the body.

Cystitis An inflammation of the bladder.

Dis-ease Imbalance in the mind, body or spirit, usually involving pain and/or discomfort.

Diuretic Having the effect of stimulating urination.

Dowager's Hump A curvature of the spine, often caused by poor posture or osteoporosis.

Drug Any chemical which alters the body, mind or emotions. It may be purchased over-the-counter or prescribed by a physician.

Dyspareunia Pain during intercourse.

Endometrium The inner layer of tissue which lines the uterus. It is released once a month during menstruation if conception does not occur. If conception does occur, it cushions the fertilized egg.

Endometriosis A form of uterine dis-ease in which the endometrium flows backward into the uterine cavity, implanting itself upon the ovaries and/or other organs.

Endorphin A chemical substance released by the brain that acts like a painkiller and adds to your sense of well-being.

Energy The force which propels you to action and supports that action.

Episiotomy An incision in the perineum to widen the vagina and speed birth.

Estrogen A female hormone that stimulates growth of estrogen dependent organs.

Excitatory Pleasure System The part of your nervous system which enables you to feel excitement and a strong sense of well-being.

Fibrositis An arthritic disorder in which there is inflammattion of the connective tissues, causing pain and stiffness.

Five Elements Theory The Taoist belief that life should be lived in accordance with the changing seasons. This is the philosophical foundation of Acupressure and Acupuncture.

Frontal headache Head pain which is concentrated in the front of the head, often a sinus headache.

Heartburn An unpleasant, burning sensation which occurs in your solar plexus, generally the result of eating too much food at one time.

Herb A plant, usually edible, which can be used for medicinal purposes.

Holistic An approach which emphasizes the whole organism, rather than focusing exclusively upon one of its aspects.

Hormone A living cell product which has a stimulating effect on cellular activity.

Hypertension Abnormally high arterial blood pressure.

Hypothalamus A glandular center which stimulates biochemical processes, like the menstrual cycle.

Immune System Body/mind resources for resisting dis-ease.

Insulin A protein hormone, secreted by the pancreas, which is essential for the processing of carbohydrates.

Inhibitory Pleasure System The part of your nervous system which enables you to feel relaxed and calm.

Insomnia Sleep problems.

Lactation The physical process of producing milk to feed a baby.

Lochia A vaginal discharge which all women experience after childbirth.

Massage One of the touch therapies.

Menopause The midlife cessation of menstruation.

Meridians The energy pathways of the body.

Modality A method of operation.

Morphine A pain-killing drug which is strongly addictive.

Nervous system Brain, spinal cord and the network of nerves which regulate and coordinate all body systems.

Neural Receptors Theorized as the Acupressure points.

Neuralgia Pain which radiates along the course of one or more nerves.

Norepinephrine (or noradrenalin) A "fight or flight" hormone (catecholamine) which elevates your blood pressure.

Nutrition The science of eating and drinking for maximum benefit.

Osteoarthritis A type of arthritis that wears away the joint cartilage. It most commonly affects the back, knees, hips and fingers.

Osteoporosis Brittle bone dis-ease which makes you prone to fractures.

Ovulation Release of an egg from one ovary on or near the fifteenth day of the menstrual cycle.

Pelvic inflammatory dis-ease An infection of the pelvic organs.

Perineum Muscles surrounding the vagina, anus and bladder opening.

Pituitary A glandular center at the base of the brain which produces the hormones to stimulate many of your body's cycles.

Placenta The organ which connects mother and developing infant during pregnancy. It filters nutrients from the mother's blood into that of the baby.

Postpartum After birth.

Premenstrual Syndrome Uncomfortable symptoms which appear in the two weeks before menstruation.

Prenatal The pregnancy period.

Progesterone A hormone secreted during the two premenstrual weeks.

Prostaglandins Fatty acids which stimulate smooth muscle contraction and affect hormone action.

Pulsation Throbbing, as in the throbbing of your heart.

Rheumatoid arthritis A form of arthritis which typically causes pain and swelling in the smaller joints, particularly the toes, fingers, wrists and ankles.

Round ligament spasm Contraction of the ligaments which support the uterus.

Shin splints Abnormal muscular tightness and pain in the legs.

Solar Plexus The pit of the stomach.

Sodium Salt.

Stress Demands upon your spiritual and physical energy.

Stress management An active program to counteract stress.

Stress reduction Limiting stress.

Tai Chi Chu'an Graceful, meditative exercises to balance the body. Taoism A philosophy stressing unity.

Thoracic Relating to the chest.

Thorax Area between the neck and the breastbone.

Tofu Soybean food which is rich in protein, calcium and other nutrients.

Tonify To increase energy.

Toxins Substances harmful to people, plants and animals.

Trauma A negative situation, such as an accident, which stresses the body.

Urinary incontinence Inability to control the flow of urine.

Vaginismus Vaginal spasm which makes coitus painful or impossible.

Vaginitis Vaginal irritation.

Varicose veins Swollen, painful veins.

Vertebrae Bones of the spine.

Vertigo Dizziness.

Visualization Forming thoughts and mental images.

APPENDIX II

INDEX OF PRESSURE POINTS

Spleen 3	Supreme White
Spleen 4	Prince's Grandson
Spleen 6	Three Yin Crossing
Spleen 12	Rushing Gate
Spleen 21	Great Enveloping
Stomach 1	Receive Tears
Stomach 3	Great Cheekbone
Stomach 13	Energy Door
Stomach 16	Breast Window
Stomach 25	Heavenly Pivot
Stomach 36	Three More Miles.
Stomach 41	Released Stream
Stomach 42	Rushing Yang
Stomach 43	Sinking Valley
Lung 1	Middle Palace
Lung 2	Cloud Gate
Lung 9	Very Great Abyss
Large Intestine 4	Great Eliminator
Large Intestine 20	Welcome Fragrance
Bladder 1	Eyes Bright
Bladder 2	Collect Bamboo
Bladder 7	Penetrate Heaven
Bladder 38	Rich for the Vitals
Bladder 42	Spiritual Soul Gate
Bladder 47	Ambition Room
Bladder 64	Capital Bone
Bladder 66	Penetrating Valley
Bladder 67	Extremity of Yin
Kidney 1	Bubbling Spring
Kidney 3	Greater Mountain Stream
Kidney 11	Transverse Bone
Kidney 22	Walking on the Verandah

Gall Bladder 1	Orbit Bone
Gall Bladder 11	Head Hole Yin
Gall Bladder 14	Yang White
Gall Bladder 20	Wind Pond
Gall Bladder 21	Shoulder Well
Gall Bladder 25	Capital Gate
Gall Bladder 30	Jumping Circle
Gall Bladder 40	Wilderness Mound
Liver 3	Supreme Rushing
Liver 6	Middle Capital
Liver 14	Gate of Hope
Heart 1	Utmost Source
Heart 7	Spirit Gate
Heart 9	Little Rushing In
Pericardium 9	Great Mound
Small Intestine 4	Wrist Bone
Small Intestine 8	Small Sea
Small Intestine 17	Heavenly Appearance
Small Intestine 19	Listening Palace
Triple Warmer 3	Middle Islet
Triple Warmer 4	Yang Pond
Triple Warmer 15	Heavenly Bone
Triple Warmer 23	Silk Bamboo Hollow
Governing Vessel 2	Loins Correspondence
Governing Vessel 4	Gate of Life
Governing Vessel 12	Body Pillar
Governing Vessel 16	Wind Palace
Governing Vessel 17	Brain Door
Governing Vessel 19	Posterior Summit
Governing Vessel 20	One Thousand Meeting Place
Conception Vessel 2	Crooked Bone
Conception Vessel 3	Utmost Middle
Conception Vessel 4	First Gate
Conception Vessel 12	Middle Duct
Conception Vessel 17	Within the Breast
Conception Vessel 24	Receiving Fluid

APPENDIX III

RECOMMENDED READINGS

Chapter One
Boston Women's Health Book Collective, *The New Our Bodies, Ourselves*, rev. 1985, $14.95. Paper.
Medical Self-Care, P.O. Box 1000, Pt. Reyes, CA 94956.
Patterson, Ann, Acupressure for Women's Health in *Women's Health Care*, edited by Weiss, Kay, Reston, 1984, $14.95.
Prudden, Bonnie, *Myotherapy: Bonnie Prudden's Complete Guide to Pain-Free Living*, Ballentine Books, 1985, $9.95.

Chapter Two
Connelly, Dianne M., *Traditional Acupuncture: The Law of the Five Elements*, The Center for Traditional Acupuncture, Inc., 1975, $8.95.
EastWest Journal, P.O. Box 6769, Syracuse, NY 13217.
Kaptchuck, Ted J., *The Web That Has No Weaver, Understanding Chinese Medicine*, Congdon and Weed, 1983, $19.95.
Serizawa, Katsusuke, *Tsubo: Vital Points for Oriental Therapy*, Japan Publications, 1976, $22.95.
Teeguarden, Iona, *Acupressure Way of Health: Jin Shin Do*, Japan Publications, Inc., 1978, $9.95.

Chapter Three
Bender, Stephanie DeGraff, *PMS: A Positive Program to Gain Control*, The Body Press, Tucson, AZ, 1986, $7.95.
Harrison, Michelle, *Self-Help for Premenstrual Syndrome*, Random House, rev. 1982, $9.95.
Hutchinson, Marcia, *Transforming Body Image*, The Crossing Press (Bookpeople), 1985, $8.95.
Kilmartin, Angela, *Cystitis*, Warner Books, 1980, $3.95.
Kitzinger, Sheila, *Woman's Experience of Sex*, Putnam, 1983, $9.95.
Lark, Susan, *Dr. Susan Lark's Premenstrual Syndrome Self-Help Book*, Forman Publishing Co., 1984, $12.95.
Madaras, Lynda et al., *Womancare*, Avon Books, 1981, $9.95.

Chapter Four
Better Babies Series, Pennypress, 1100 Twenty-third Avenue East, Seattle, WA 98112, $.50-$1.00.
Ashford, Janet Isaacs, ed., *Birth Stories: The Experience Remembered*, The Crossing Press (Bookpeople), 1985, $7.95.

Baldwin, Rahima, et al., *Pregnant Feelings*, Celestial Arts, 1986, $10.95.

Edwards, Margot, et al., *Reclaiming Birth: History and Heroines of American Childbirth Reform*, The Crossing Press (Bookpeople), 1985, $8.95.

Gold, Cybele, et al., *Joyous Childbirth*, And/Or Press, 1977, $8.95.

Herzfeld, Judith, *Sense and Sensibililty in Childbirth: A Guide to Negotiating Supportive Obstetrical Care*, Summit, 1985, $12.95.

Huggins, Kathleen, *The Nursing Mother's Companion*, Harvard Common Press, 1986, $6.96.

Inkeles, Gordon, *Massage and Peaceful Pregnancy*, Perigee, 1983, $8.95.

Chapter Five

Gach, Michael, *Acu-Yoga*, Japan Press, 1981, $10.95.

Gach, Michael, *The Bum Back Book*, Celestial Arts, 1985, $7.95.

Greenwood, Sadja, *Menopause, Naturally*, Volcano Press, 1984, $10.00.

Painter, Charlotte, *Gifts of Age*, Chronicle Books, 1986, $14.95.

Phillips, Alice et al., *A Practical Guide for Independent Living for Older People*, Pacific Search Press, 222 Dexter Avenue North, Seattle, WA 98109, $6.95.

Porcino, Jane, *Growing Older, Getting Better*, Addison-Wesley, 1983, $8.95.

Prudden, Bonnie, *Myotherapy, Bonnie Prudden's Complete Guide to Pain-Free Living*, Ballentine Books, 1985, $9.95.

Reitz, Rosetta, *Menopause: A Positive Approach*, Chilton, 1978, $6.95.

Seaman, Barbara, et al., *Women and the Crisis in Sex Hormones*, Rawson Associates, 1977, $12.95.

INDEX

A

Abdominal pain, 20
Abraham, Dr. Guy, 43
Acne, 21, 38, 69
    Premenstrual Acne, Acupressure
    Points for, 69
Acupressure
    Origins, 4
    Self-treatment, 7
    Asian view of, 16-36
    Western view of, 5, 12-13
Acupuncture, 4
Adele bed, 100
Adrenals, 69, 110
Affirmations, 10, 66, 79
Aging, 18, see Chapter Five
Alfalfa, 102
Allergies, 18, also see Sinus dis-ease
Althea, 118
American Heart Association, 127
Androgens, 69, 110
Androstanedione, 110
Anger, 18
Angina, 12
Anise seed, 52, 106
Anxiety, 4, 13, 50, 106
Apathy, 19
Arthritis, 128
Asthma, 21
Autumn, 21

B

Backache, 17, 64, 75, 88, 90
    Acupressure Points for Backache and
    Muscular Pain, 65
    Acupressure Points for Backache and
    Muscular Stiffness, 90
Bath Products, Natural, 131
Bender, Stephanie DeGraff, 42
Beta blockers, 125
Beverages for Lactation, 106
Biofeedback, 4
Birkenstock shoes, 94
Birthing, 75, 96-102
    Acupressure Points for, 97
Birthing positions, 100
Black Bean Tonic, 73
Bladder meridian, 17, 23
Bladder 1, 51, 83, 87, 130, 142

Bladder 2, 83, 87, 130, 142
Bladder 7, 142
Bladder 38, 49, 65, 90, 142
Bladder 42, 90, 142
Bladder 47, 60, 90, 142
Bladder 64, 120, 122, 142
Bladder 66, 115, 119, 120, 142
Bladder 67, 97, 142
Bladder changes at menopause, 110, 117
    Acupressure Points for Bladder
    Health, 120
Bladder infections, 17
Blood pressure, see Hypertension Blood
    pressure equipment, page 125
Bonding, 102, 107
Bone health, 17, 110, 121-122
Boneset, 84
Bong-han, Dr. Kim, 16
Borning bed, 100
Braxton-Hicks contractions, 96
Breastfeeding, see Nursing Breast
    engorgement, 102
Breast tenderness, 77, 81
    Acupressure Points for, 81
Breath, 12, 21, 94
Bresler, Dr. David, 13
Brewer, Dr. Tom, 92
Brewer's yeast, 127
Bronchitis, 21
Budoff, Dr. Penny, 43
Burdock root, 55
Bursitis, 18

C

Cabbage, 52
Calcium, 57, 121, 123
    and Bone Health, 122
Canker sores, 20
Cardiovascular system, 110, 125, 127
Carpal tunnel syndrome, 50, 88, 92
Carrot juice, 106, 134
Cat Cow, 68
Catecholamines, 96
Cayenne, 84
Cervix, 40
Chest constriction, 12
Cholesterol, 12, 125, 127
Christie, Agatha, 111
Circulation, 17, 19, 43, 128, 129, 130, 131

Cobra Pose, 68
Cod liver oil, 127
Cohosh, 72
Coitus, see Sex Colds, 21, 84
   Natural Cold Remedies, 84
Cold hands and feet, 17
Comfrey, 104
Complexion, see Skin Congestion,
   see nasal congestion Conception
   Vessel meridian, 21, 34
Conception Vessel 2, 62, 63, 143
Conception Vessel 3, 74, 143
Conception Vessel 4, 60, 143
Conception Vessel 12, 86, 143
Conception Vessel 17, 126, 143
Conception Vessel 24, 69, 130, 143
Constipation, 21, 57, 83, 86, 132, 134
   Acupressure Points for, 135
   Acupressure Points for Heartburn
   and, 86 Natural Remedies for, 134
Contingency Plan for PMS, 47
Cotton root, 72
Couchgrass, 72
Cramps, see Period pain Creativity, 19
Cross Stretch, 67
Cystitis, 61

D

Dalton, Dr. Katharina, 41
Delayed menstruation, 21
Depression, 12, 13, 19, 50, 88, 111, 123
Diabetes, 12, 20
Diaphragm, 61
Diarrhea, 21
Dick-Read, Grantly, 96
Diet, see Nutrition Digestion, 18, 20, 21
Dill, 106
Dis-ease, 5, 16, 36
Diuretics, 52, 92
   Natural Diuretics, 52
Dizziness, 43, 45, 50
Donden, Yeshi, 7
Dong quai, 114
Drugs, 4, 45
Dyspareunia, 61, 117
Dystocia, 96

E

Earache, 17, 50
Ears, 17, 23

Earth element, 20
Eating disorders, 20
Eczema, 21
Edema, 92
Elements, see Five Elements Theory
Emotion, 18-21, 36, 77
Emotional Symptoms of PMS, Acupressure
   Points for, 48-49
Endometrium, 40
Endometriosis, 61
Endorphins, 13, 46
Energy, 4, 5, 6, 16, 17, 36
Engorgement, 107
Episiotomy,
   Healing an, 104
   The Question About, 101
Estrogen, 39, 40, 110, 117
Estrogen replacement hormones, 111,
   113, 116, 121
   Pros and Cons of Using, 116
Evening Primrose Oil, 46
Excitatory pleasure center, 13
Exercise, 64, 88, 92, 121, 123,
   127, 128, 129
Exercises for the Wrists, 93
Extra meridians, 21
Extra point on the ear, 97

F

Fatigue, 38, 43, 52, 53, 77, 79, 96,
   106, 107
   Premenstrual Fatigue, Acupressure
   Points for, 53
   Prenatal Fatigue, Acupressure Points
   for, 80
Fear, 17
Feet, 94
Fertility, 20
Fight-or flight-reflex, 12
Fire element, 19,
First stage labor, 96
Five Elements Theory, 16, 17-36
Flapping Wings, 67
Fluid retention, see Water Retention
Flushing, 114
Foot Care in Late Pregnancy, 94
Frequent urination, 75, 117

G

Gall Bladder meridian, 18, 24
Gall Bladder 1, 87, 130, 143
Gall Bladder 2, 76
Gall Bladder 9, 76
Gall Bladder 11, 83, 143
Gall Bladder 14, 143
Gall Bladder 20, 87, 105, 143
Gall Bladder 21, 97, 143
Gall Bladder 25, 91, 143
Gall Bladder 30, 62, 65, 90, 143
Gall Bladder 40, 103, 143
Gamma-linoleic acid, 46
Garlic, 52
Ginger, 72, 104
Ginseng, 72
Golden seal, 72
Glucose, 54
Governing Vessel meridian, 34
Governing Vessel 2, 59, 62, 65, 90,
    103, 143
Governing Vessel 4, 65, 90, 103, 143
Governing Vessel 12, 65, 143
Governing Vessel 16, 143
Governing Vessel 17, 143
Governing Vessel 19, 143
Governing Vessel 20, 80, 143
Greenwood, Dr. Sadja, 114
Grief, 21, 127
Grounding Yourself with the Positive
    Pregnancy Stance, 89

H

Hair, 17
Harrison, Dr. Michelle, 42
Headaches, 18, 21, 45, 50, 87, 123
    Acupressure Points for Headache
    Relief, 87
    Natural Headache Remedies, 87
Health Is..., 5
Heart meridian, 19, 26
Heart 1, 126, 143
Heart 7, 48, 126, 143
Heart 9, 143
Heart dis-ease, 19, 26, 124-127
    Acupressure Points to Tonify the
    Heart, 126
    Taking Heart, 127
Heartburn, 77, 83

Herbs, 4, 7, 72
    to Avoid When You are Pregnant or
    Nursing a Baby, 72
Hormones, 40, 41
Hot Flashes, 110, 113
    Acupressure Points for Relief of, 115
    Herbal Treatment of, 114
How to Work With Acupressure Points, 6
Hypertension, 12, 125
Hypoglycemia, 20, 41, 43, 54
Hypothalmus, 113

I

Indecision, 18
Indigestion, 38, 57, 78
    Acupressure Points for Period Pain
    and Indigestion, 58
Infertility, 17, 20
Inhibitory pleasure center, 13
Insomnia, 12, also see Relaxation
Insufficient Vaginal Lubrication
    Acupressure Points for, 63
Insulin, 54
Intercourse pain, see Dyspareunia
Involution, 102, 105
Iron, 123
Irritability, 123

J

Jalap, 134
Janeway, Elizabeth, 123
Joint stiffness, 12, 18, 129
    Acupressure Points for Joint Pain and
    Stiffness, 129
Joy, 19

K

Kegel exercises, 101, 104, 117, 118
Kidneys, 17, 61, 64
Kidney meridian, 17, 21, 22
Kidney Rub, 73
Kidney 1, 51, 53, 63, 76, 103, 119,
    122, 142
Kidney 2, 76
Kidney 3, 51, 53, 63, 74, 115, 119,
    120, 122, 142
Kidney 4, 76
Kidney 7, 76
Kidney 11, 119, 142
Kidney 22, 53, 80, 81, 105, 142

L

La Leche League, 107
Labor, 96,
Lactation, see Nursing
Large Intestine meridian, 21, 32
Large Intestine 4, 76, 97, 135, 142
Large Intestine 10, 76
Large Intestine 11, 74, 76, 142
Large Intestine 15, 80, 142
Large Intestine 20, 69, 130, 142
Lark, Dr. Susan, 38
Late Summer, 20
Laxatives, 57, 134
Lemon, 106
Letdown of milk, 105
Li Shih-chen, 36
Lipoproteins, 125, 127
Life Nerve Stretch, 68
Ligaments, 18
Liver meridian, 18, 25
Liver 3, 78, 105, 143
Liver 6, 97, 143
Liver 14, 143
Low back pain, see Backache
Low blood sugar, see Hypoglycemia
Lovage root, 131
Lubrication, see Vaginal Lubrication
Lung 1, 49, 83, 95, 105, 142
Lung 2, 83, 95, 142
Lung 7, 76
Lung 9, 95, 142
Lung 11, 76
Lung meridian, 21, 33

M

Magnesium, 54, 57, 123
Marshmallow root, 118
Massage, 4, 102
Menopause, see Chapter Five Menstrual
  cramps, see Period pain
Menstrual cycle, 20
Menstrual Cycle Events, 39
Menstruation, delayed, 21
Metal element, 21
Meridians, 16, 19,
  charts, 22-35
  imbalance in, 36
Migraines, 13
Milk ejection reflex, 105
Montagu, Dr. Ashley, 106

Mood swings, 20, 43
Morning sickness, see Nausea
Motherwort, 72, 114
Mullein, 55
Muscles, 18, 38
Muscular spasms, 18
Musculoskeletal pain and stiffness, 13, 124
  128-129 Acupressure Points for Back-
  ache and Muscular Pain, 65

N

Nasal congestion, 50
  Acupressure Points for, 83
Nausea, 38, 75, 77
  Acupressure Points for Prenatal
  Nausea and Indigestion, 78
Natural Diuretics, 52
Nettle tea, 87
Nervous system, 12, 13, 45, 92, 113
Neural receptors, 13
Newton, Dr. Niles, 110
Norepinephrine, 12
Numbness, 43
Nursing, 74, 105-107
Nursing, Acupressure Points for, 105
Nutrition, 36, 45, 47, 69, 75, 76, 77,
  86, 127

O

Oil of primrose, 46
Olfactory nerve, 50
Osteoarthritis, 128
Osteoporosis, 121-122
Ovarian hormones, 40
Ovarian regression, 110
Ovulation, 20
Oxytocin, 105

P

Pain, 4, 12-13, 17, 36, 43, 96
Pain at intercourse, see Dyspareunia
Painter, Charlotte, 123
Panic, 12
Pap smears, 7, 110
Papaya leaves, 131
Parsley, 52
Pelvic exams, 7
Pelvic inflammatory dis-ease, 61
Pelvic pain, 61

Pelvic tension, 61,
  Acupressure Points to Relieve, 62
Pennyroyal, 72
Peppermint, 77, 106
Pericardium meridian, 19, 27
Pericardium 6, 76
Pericardium 7, 103, 127, 143
Pericardium 8, 76
Pericardium 9, 143
Perineum,
  Caring for the Intact, 104
Period pain, 38, 41, 57, 60, 61
  Acupressure Points for Period Pain
    and Indigestion, 58
  Point Series for, 60
Phobias, 17
Phosphorus, 122
Placenta, 75, 102,
Plaque, 125
Pomeranz, Dr. Bruce, 13
Porcino, Jane, 111, 123
Positive mental attitude, 7, 10, 45
Positive Nutrition for PMS, 46
Positive Pregnancy Stance, 89
Postpartum pain, 75
Postpartum recovery, 102-105
  Acupressure Points for, 105
Potassium, 52
Precautions (in using Acupressure), 7
  Acupressure Points to Avoid During
    Pregnancy, 76
Preconception Period, 72-74
  Acupressure Points for the, 74
Pregnancy, see Chapter Four
Premenstrual Syndrome, 13, 20, see
  Chapter 3
Preventive Medicine Research Institute, 12
Progesterone, 40-41
Prostaglandins, 41, 43, 46,
Protein, 75, 77, 82, 92
  Convenient, Inexpensive Protein
    Foods, 82
Pryor, Karen, 106

Q
Quick Energy Foods, 55

R
Raspberry leaf, 77
Reitz, Rosetta, 114

Relaxation, 8, 12, 13, 21, 125
Reproduction, 72, see Chapter Four
Rue, 72

S
Safflower oil, 131
Sage, 72, 102
Salt, 17, 41, 45, 52
Saint John's Wort, 72
Selye, Dr. Hans, 12, 96
Senility, 123
Serotonin, 46
Service Corps of Retired Executives, 123
Sesame oil, 131
Sex, 17, 19, 20, 57, 61, 110, 117
  Pain during, see Dyspareunia
Shakti shoes, 94
Shiatsu, 4
Shortness of breath, 94
  Acupressure Points to Relieve, 95
Sinus dis-ease, 21, 50, 83
Skin, 19, 21, 130, 131
  also see Acne Small Intestine meridi-
    an, 19, 28
Small Intestine 4, 69, 143
Small Intestine 7, 76
Small Intestine 8, 97, 143
Small Intestine 10, 76
Small Intestine 17, 143
Small Intestine 19, 143
Soap bulb, 131
Sore nipples, 107, also see Breast
  tenderness
Spearmint, 77, 106
Spinal problems, 18
Spleen meridian, 20, 31
Spleen 1, 76
Spleen 2, 76
Spleen 3, 48, 56, 58, 74, 78, 103, 142
Spleen 4, 56, 142
Spleen 6, 60, 76, 142
Spleen 12, 59, 60, 142
Spleen 21, 91, 142
Spring, 18
Squawgrss, 72
Stitch in the side, 91
  Acupressure Points for a, 91
Stomach meridian, 20, 30
Stomach 1, 51, 87, 142
Stomach 3, 83, 130, 142

Stomach 4, 76
Stomach 13, 81, 105, 142
Stomach 16, 81, 105, 142
Stomach 25, 86, 135, 142
Stomach 36, 53, 56, 76, 142
Stomach 41, 142
Stomach 42, 48, 56, 58, 78, 103, 142
Stomach 43, 115, 142
Stomach 45, 76
Stomach/abdominal pain, 20
Storch, Dr. Marcia, 45
Stress, 5, 7, 12, 13, 14, 17, 43, 113, 124
  reduction, 8, 12
Stretching, 66-68, 88
  A Guide for Stretching, 67
Summer, 19
Surwit, Dr. Richard, 12
Sweet craving, 20, 38, 54, 55
  Acupressure Points for Premenstrual
  Sweet Craving, 56
Sweet marjoram, 106
Swelling, 50, 92
Sympathy, 20,

T

Tai Chi Chu'an, 111
Taking Charge of PMS Emotions, 45
Tansy, 72
Taoism, 16
Tendonitis, 18
Tendons, 18
Tension, 12, 88, 132
  along meridians, 17-21
Tofu, 82
Trauma, 13
Triple Warmer meridian, 19, 29,
Triple Warmer 3, 80, 85, 115, 143
Triple Warmer 4, 143
Triple Warmer 7, 74, 143
Triple Warmer 15, 85, 90, 143
Triple Warmer 23, 143
Trytophan, 46

U

Ulcers, 20,
Urinary tract infections, 17

V

Vaginal changes at menopause, 110, 117

Vaginal irritation, 38, 117
  Acupressure Points to Promote
  Vaginal Tone, 119
Vaginal lubrication, 61, 117
  Acupressure Points for
  Insufficient, 63
Vaginismus, 61
Valerian, 72
Valois, Pamela, 123
Vegetable Stew, 46
Vervain, 72
Vision, 18
Visualization, 8, 79
Vitamin A, 123, 124
Vitamin B complex, 45, 105, 123
Vitamin B6, 42, 43, 92
Vitamin C, 123, 127
Vitamin D, 121, 122
Vitamin E, 104, 113, 127, 131
Vomiting, 20

W

Water retention, 17, 41, 45, 50, 52, 64
Water retention, Acupressure Points for, 51
Water, 17, 22-23
Water Wheel, 67
Wheat germ, 104
Winter, 17
Wood, 18
Wrists, Exercises for the, 93

Y

Yeast infection, 20
Yerba Santa tea, 87
Yoga, 88, 102, 128
Your Earth Element, 20
Your Fire Element, 19
Your Metal Element, 21
Your Water Element, 17
Your Wood Element, 18
Yucca, 131